Taking the IPC Forward

Engaging with the International Primary Curriculum

Edited by
Mary Hayden and Jeff Thompson

A John Catt Publication

First Published 2012

by John Catt Educational Ltd,
12 Deben Mill Business Centre, Old Maltings Approach,
Melton, Woodbridge IP12 1BL

Tel: +44 (0) 1394 389850 Fax: +44 (0) 1394 386893
Email: enquiries@johncatt.com
Website: www.johncatt.com

ISBN: 978 1 908095 48 0

eISBN: 978 1 908095 49 7

Set and designed by John Catt Educational Limited

Printed and bound in Great Britain
by Ashford Colour Press

Contents

Taking the IPC Forward

About the contributors

Nicola Cooper taught first in the UK and then in The Netherlands, where she was a class teacher before becoming ESL coordinator at Joppenhof International School. She completed language teaching qualifications and an MA in applied linguistics, and her developing interest for mother tongue maintenance and programming resulted in a number of initiatives to address the social, emotional and language needs of students. Nicola is currently vice-principal of academics at UWC Maastricht primary school, and intends to pursue her passion for language teaching through a whole college role.

Catherine Copeland is founding principal of UWC Maastricht. Her teaching career began in Canada and posts in London, Amsterdam and Maastricht followed. Since entering educational management, her interests have involved socio-cultural linguistics, change management, curriculum quality, assessment and looking for learning. She is researching public-private partnerships in hybrid schools for her doctoral studies. Catherine's passion for children drives her to seek her own excellence in leadership and innovative education. The UWC Maastricht provides the backdrop for her learning within a mission and value set she shares with her community of inspiring colleagues.

Malcolm Davis is director of the International School of Bremen. He entered international education in 1981 having learnt the craft of teaching in UK comprehensive schools. He has taught and led in elementary, middle and IB Diploma sections of schools. Malcolm has also been particularly active in teacher education in Eastern Europe and has written widely on approaches to teaching philosophy and Islamic history and culture. In addition he presently works closely with the IB in assessing philosophy and history.

Barbara Deveney has had teaching and leadership experience in international primary schools for 30 years. She has worked in special needs, as a class teacher and headteacher, and as an 'ESL in the mainstream' teacher-trainer. Barbara has lived and worked in Kuwait, Thailand and Vietnam and is currently headteacher of an international primary school in Western Siberia. She has a particular interest in the impact of culture on learning, which was the focus for her master's degree research.

Janet Harwood is an experienced special education and technology specialist. Currently working as a vice-principal of UWC Maastricht, The Netherlands, Janet has held posts both nationally in Canada and internationally in Europe for over 20 years. She has contributed to the development of digital testing, evidence-based learning, and data analysis in her present capacity. At this time, Janet is investigating international-mindedness in her doctoral studies.

Dr Mary Hayden is Director of the Centre for the study of Education in an International Context (CEIC) at the University of Bath, and editor of the Journal of Research in International Education. Her teaching, publishing and research supervision focus particularly on international schools and international education. She is a trustee of the Alliance for International Education, a member of the IPC and IMYC Advisory Board, and academic advisor to the International Leadership and Management Programme (ILMP).

Tracey Kelly is assistant head of Shell Education Services, based in The Netherlands, delivering Shell's education policies to thousands of Shell employees worldwide including the central and strategic management of 10 Shell schools. Following teacher training and a master's degree in education, Tracey worked in schools and organisations in the UK and abroad. She is a strong advocate of the UK national literacy strategy, and is also particularly interested in how neuroscience can be leveraged to inform and develop best practice in learning.

Peter le Noble taught Dutch language and literature in Dutch secondary schools. He was headmaster of primary schools in The Netherlands and the Dutch Antilles before joining Shell as headmaster of Panaga School in Brunei. He was subsequently appointed head of education for Shell International in The Hague, and was responsible for setting up and maintaining educational quality in the Shell primary schools throughout the world. Shell engaged Fieldwork Education to provide education services for these schools, which eventually led to the development of the IPC. Peter was education adviser for Shell International from 1987 to 2001.

Steven Mark is director of the International Primary Curriculum. His education experience includes many years as a teacher and school leader in Scotland, The Netherlands and Germany. Steven has a great range of experience working with both national and international schools, and has spoken at conferences and delivered professional development programmes for educators worldwide. He is currently writing a book about developing international-mindedness, which he thinks may well become the key skill for 21st century citizens.

Joanne Marshall has worked both in the UK and internationally for the past 16 years and is currently head of Year 1 at Al Khor International School Qatar. She was part of the leadership team that introduced the IPC into the British International School of Jeddah. She is also studying for a master's degree, with a focus on the IPC and its increasing popularity in state schools in England and Wales.

Richard Mast is the founding head of Léman International School in China. His 40-year career in education includes teacher, IB MYP coordinator, principal and school head in China, Sweden and Australia. His focus has been on learning, curriculum and mechanisms for improvement of education, including developing innovative courses for secondary schooling as well as participation in the development of ESL in the Mainstream. He is currently working on a standards-based reporting model.

Professor Yolande Muschamp is Dean of the School of Education, Social Work and Community Learning and Development at the University of Dundee. The School delivers both undergraduate and postgraduate teacher education programmes and is the first in Scotland to offer the International Baccalaureate Educator Certificates. Her research explores primary education and, in particular, pedagogy and curriculum reform. Her current focus is the impact of the continental European didactics tradition on the pedagogies found within Scottish primary schools.

Jayne Pletser is a doctoral student with research interests in the field of international education and learning diversity. Jayne has been involved in international education in Belgium, the Democratic Republic of the Congo and The Netherlands, where she has held teaching posts, school leadership positions and educational advisory roles. Jayne has been involved with the IPC as a school director, a member of the IPC accreditation team and as a freelance IPC course facilitator both in the UK and The Netherlands.

Graeme Scott works at the International School of Bangkok as deputy head of school for learning. He was primary principal at The International School of The Hague when it became the first school in the world to be accredited by IPC at mastering level. Prior to that, Graeme was head of a UK primary school and held leadership positions in Dubai and Hong Kong. He has also worked as an associate for Fieldwork Education, delivering keynotes and facilitating workshops.

Martin Skelton was first a teacher and subsequently a headteacher of two schools. He co-founded Fieldwork Education with the aim of helping teachers and schools improve learning, and continues to work with both around the world. He was founding director of the IPC and responsible for its design. He is committed to learning that develops people to live in the 21st century, and believes that international-mindedness is as important a part of the mix as any other 'subject'.

Dr Estelle Tarry is a senior lecturer in education at the University of Northampton. She teaches on undergraduate and postgraduate courses, including supporting international PhD students whose research focus is comparative education. Previously she was head of international schools in Sri Lanka, Thailand and The Netherlands. This experience has led her to develop the University of Northampton Certificate for Teaching Assistants in an International Context, supporting the teaching and learning of primary school children in international schools.

Professor Jeff Thompson teaches, supervises, researches and publishes through the Centre for the study of Education in an International Context (CEIC) of the University of Bath, in areas relating specifically to international schools and international education. He has worked closely for many years with the International Baccalaureate and, more recently, the IPC and IMYC

– for which he is chair of the Advisory Board. He was founding editor for the Journal of Research in International Education and is chair of the Alliance for International Education.

Mary van der Heijden worked as headteacher in one of the first schools to implement the IPC in 2000, and has also worked as an IPC trainer regularly since 2006. Her experience of more than 30 years as a teacher, headteacher, trainer, consultant and, more recently, researcher and writer has led her to many different parts of the globe. She is currently vice-principal for curriculum at the United World College of South East Asia in Singapore.

Henk van Hout taught in both secondary and primary education before accepting the headship of the Netherlands School in Lagos. Subsequent appointments included head of the Shell School in Heliopolis, Cairo, deputy headmaster in Panaga School in Brunei and, after returning to The Netherlands, director of the primary school of the Haagsche Schoolvereeniging. He later became general director of the Foundation with shared responsibility for the primary department of the International School of the Hague. Henk has a master's degree in educational superintendence. In 2007 he rejoined Shell as head of education services in The Hague.

Andrew Wigford is director of TIC Recruitment and Training, a UK-based recruitment company that deals exclusively with international schools. He has been involved in international education for over 25 years, and has taught in the UK, Germany, Colombia and Austria. His last position was as head of primary at Vienna International School. He has a master's degree in international education and was director of the International Primary Curriculum between 2002 and 2006.

Foreword

We were delighted to be asked last year to commission and edit a collection of chapter contributions from those involved in teaching, leading, managing, training, recruiting and development activities relating to the International Primary Curriculum (IPC). Our reasons for being so pleased to accept this invitation were related, in part, to the strong reputation that the programme has established in the relatively short period since its creation, a reputation of which we had become acutely aware during our own teaching and researching in the field of international education. Having previously been invited to be members of the Advisory Board for the IPC, we both continue to enjoy that role – as critical friends and reviewers. Additionally, we believed that, in encouraging those who have first hand knowledge of IPC implementation in a variety of schools across the world to share that experience through their writing, we would learn, in more general educational terms, what lies behind the success of what is arguably the fastest growing international education programme in the world at present, offered in over 1500 schools in some 80 countries as at October 2012.

As will be evident from the first section of contributions, the origins of the IPC lay in meeting a specific set of curriculum challenges that arose from catering for the needs of children educated in Shell's schools around the world. With encouragement and support from Shell, Fieldwork Education was tasked with taking forward the development of the curriculum, and in 2001 the first set of materials became available to schools for what was by then the International Primary Curriculum. Those materials were the outcome of research into the availability of existing curricula for the primary phase of education throughout the world, together with the identified needs of primary schools interested and involved in the project at its inception. Martin Skelton and Graham Reeves, writing in 2001 about the initial process of IPC development, explained clearly the criteria that would need to be met if the curriculum were ultimately to be judged successful in achieving its goals. The curriculum, they said, would need to:

- be genuinely international;
- be based on the central importance of children's learning;
- provide teachers with as much time as possible to think about teaching their own classes;
- respond to recent ideas about learning, particularly through brain research;
- help parents to help their children to learn;
- be enjoyable for teachers to teach and engaging and fun for children; and
- facilitate the extension of knowledge, skills and understanding, to develop personal attributes and to support an international perspective in a way that responds to revised ideas about learning.

An ambitious set of goals indeed!

In commissioning colleagues who have first hand knowledge of the IPC to write for this book from their experiences, we hoped that views would emerge concerning both the appropriateness of those criteria more than ten years on, and the extent to which they can be   and have been – realised in practice. We were also interested to see if ideas might emerge about ways in which the curriculum could develop in future. Maybe the time is ripe, in reviewing the original criteria, to affirm those that have clearly been successful and are essential ingredients for the framework and to add any others demanded by the context of current changes taking place worldwide. The outcome has been a collection of vignettes of personal experience with the IPC, borne out of engagement with the programme from a variety of perspectives. All our contributors have sought to share with readers their open views and practical experiences, in ways intended to contribute to the development of the IPC by those involved in its implementation in schools and by Fieldwork in supporting them. They have thereby fulfilled the best traditions of being critical friends and the issues they raise will surely inform the future evolution of the programme.

We have grouped the contributions into four major sections which define the overall structure for the book and thereby give an indication of the major themes emerging from the separate chapters. In **Part A**, contributions are grouped together from those involved in the origins of the curriculum, with an overview from its current director. One message strongly repeated in any discussion of the IPC is the flexibility of the curriculum framework that enables (and encourages) teachers to incorporate local – even national – requirements into their overall planning of students' learning. Originating as it did from the needs of the Shell schools, in which Dutch, English and international curriculum features were brought together, the flexibility and adaptability that were clear characteristics of the programme enabled national and international schools alike to incorporate the IPC into their planning for student learning at the primary phase.

Part B is entitled *The Curriculum Context*, for what the IPC offers is a strong framework within which the needs of students and teachers can be brought together in generating the detailed arrangements that best support student learning in the specific contexts in which it takes place. How fit-for-purpose is that framework, and how successful will it be in meeting the changing demands of primary education in future? Theoretical and practical considerations are included and clear views concerning the flexibility that it offers to both students and teachers are echoed from the previous section, together with the issue of authenticity of the student experience that it encourages. The notion of international-mindedness and its realisation through such a curriculum framework, together with the place for subject knowledge and interdisciplinarity within the structure, are featured along with the challenges of presenting what may be perceived as an essentially western construct within an international context.

Part C, *Teaching and Learning through the IPC*, highlights the fundamental focus of the programme – student learning and the pedagogic necessities that have to be addressed in meeting the exacting demands of learning in such a wide range of contexts. Student perceptions of their own learning, teacher and parental views on learning and motivation, and the challenges of recruiting those responsible for designing and supporting the learning in schools, are all included. Crucial messages about the importance of including all stakeholders in the process of understanding and supporting student learning emerge from those contributing in this section.

Whilst the central emphasis of the IPC is on student learning, there is strong evidence of the effect that incorporating the IPC framework into schools can have on the whole institution. Contributions from those in school leadership positions attest to the value of the programme in supporting the process of whole school reform and development, and these are included in **Part D**. Maintenance and improvement of quality is important, not only for the schools and the confidence of the communities that each one serves, but also in assuring standards across all schools, especially as the programme continues to experience rapid growth in numbers of schools participating.

After all chapters were written we invited Martin Skelton, in every sense the person behind the creation, development and inspiration of the IPC, to add his own comments regarding the current and future prospects for the curriculum and to identify the major trends and changes with which it will need to engage in its continuing success. We are grateful to him, and to all our authors, for the time and effort they have devoted to reflecting upon their engagement in the programme and for their readiness to express the outcomes of their practical experience in the chapters they have contributed. They have, without exception, exercised understanding and patience in equal measure with the demands of the editors and for that we are especially grateful. Our thanks are due also to our colleagues at John Catt, who have been supportive at every step of the way. Finally, to all those students, teachers, parents, administrators and trainers who have contributed, often unwittingly no doubt through their valuable work in schools, to the outcomes that have made possible this exploration of the IPC, we offer our gratitude and all good wishes for success in their continuing endeavours.

Mary Hayden
Jeff Thompson

Part A
Origins and Background

Chapter 1

The making of the IPC: a personal view

Peter le Noble

A historical introduction

When, in 1980, I started to work in the Panaga Shell school in Brunei, as teacher and head of the Dutch stream, the way the school was organised took me by surprise. Here were two schools (an English primary school and a Dutch primary school) under one roof, but very much apart. The only integration I noticed took place after school hours, during activities for the children: some run by parents and some by teachers. Other things that struck me were the low pupil-teacher ratio and the wealth of books and education materials available in the school. Ordering of new material was never a problem; quite a change from what was then common practice in state schools in The Netherlands and the UK, where every penny counted.

I was also surprised to see very few British children older than nine in the English stream. This was the result of Shell's education policy whereby British parents were allowed to have their children in a UK boarding school from the age of nine, with the guarantee that Shell would continue to pay for boarding up to and including A level examinations – even if the parents were transferred to the UK during that period. This system made the education of British expatriate children expensive, as Shell reimbursed boarding school fees while continuing to provide primary education facilities locally so as to offer choice to the British parents. In the 1980s, Shell's expatriate workforce consisted mainly of British and Dutch employees: 45% were British, 45% Dutch and 10% others. Apart from teachers who were single, family postings were the norm at that time with very few exceptions.

In 1985 I moved on to Gabon in Africa, after five happy years in Brunei. Shell had two schools in Gabon: quite a large one in Gamba where operations were taking place, and a small one in Port Gentil where the head office was located. The school in Port Gentil consisted of an English stream and a Dutch stream; in Gamba French primary education was also available. I was head of both schools, and flew every Wednesday from Gamba to Port Gentil for meetings with teachers, pupils, parents and the Shell human resources department – a unique experience! Education offered in the Shell schools in Gabon was very much the same as in the Shell school in Brunei, which was not surprising as the curriculum and school materials were exactly the same in all Shell schools. This was clearly to the advantage of both Shell children and Shell teachers in moving from one Shell school to another.

Consistency across the Shell schools was established during the annual headteachers' conferences organised by Shell International and led by the two education advisors from Shell, alternately held in the Shell Centres in London and The Hague. During these conferences, decisions were taken on curriculum changes (within the framework of the English and Dutch national curricula) and all other issues relevant for the next school year and/or for the longer term. The representatives of the English and Dutch departments met separately with their respective colleagues during each conference. Only in the afternoon of the final day was a combined session held between all the representatives, during which decisions made during the week were exchanged and general issues such as arrangements for annual school holidays were discussed and agreed.

In 1987 I was appointed education advisor to Shell International in The Hague, to be responsible for the Dutch Shell schools abroad, and for education advice to Dutch Shell parents, to Shell parents of all other nationalities (except the British Shell parents) and to Shell operating companies. My counterpart in London was Janet Snow, who gave education advice to British parents and had responsibility for the English Shell schools abroad. We both had to provide input to the planning and recruitment of teachers and to the company's education policy as part of the general human resources policy for expatriates.

Shortly after my appointment in The Hague, the Dutch Government decided to make a subsidy available for Dutch schools abroad through an NGO: Stichting NOB (Foundation for Dutch Education Abroad). This organisation acted as a school advisory board for all Dutch schools abroad and provided excellent educational services in return for the government grant. Acceptance of the grant had as a consequence that the participating school was subject to regular government inspections. Shell International saw this as an opportunity rather than a threat and, on behalf of Shell, I signed a contract with SNOB for all the Dutch Shell schools abroad and, also on behalf of Shell, I accepted a place on the board of SNOB.

This arrangement for the Dutch Shell schools evoked in Shell a discussion on arrangements in the English Shell schools, and it was felt that similar arrangements to those in the Dutch schools should be explored. The British government was not even considering the introduction of government subsidies for British schools abroad, therefore some school advisory services in the UK were asked to make a proposal for the provision of similar services as in the Dutch schools. After careful consideration, Education Relocation Services (ERA) was awarded the contract for boarding school advice to (British) parents, while Fieldwork Education won the contract for Shell schools guidance, the organisation of the English National Curriculum Standard Assessment Tasks (SATs) and inspection visits, the recruitment of teachers and the organisation of the headteachers' conferences.

Soon after, in the early nineties, Shell made a crucial change in its recruitment policies. The new slogan was diversity and regional recruitment, which meant that emphasis would no longer be on the recruitment of British/Dutch employees but rather on the best person for the job, irrespective of nationality. This had an instant effect on the student population in the Shell schools: the numbers in the Dutch streams decreased slowly but surely, while the numbers in the English streams increased as they included children for whom English was not their mother tongue. In two years' time, in some classes in the English streams, there were hardly any British children left. Yet they all had to learn about the Tudors, the Windsors and the Pennine Chain, and sit the SATs.

The beginnings of the IPC

It was then that I started to brainstorm with Martin Skelton and David Playfoot (joint directors of Fieldwork) on a more effective and relevant truly international curriculum for our schools, which would reflect the moves towards internationalisation of the Shell expatriate workforce. Since the development of a new curriculum for Shell schools was not in Fieldwork's contract with Shell, the first discussions with Fieldwork were held in secret as if we were partners in crime. When we had a clearer view of what we wanted, we presented the idea to Shell and were given approval for a fact-finding journey to a number of well-established international schools across the world, in order to observe how these schools tackled the challenges of having many nationalities in one class with a diverse educational background. Graham Reeves of Fieldwork made that journey and returned with a bag full of facts and ideas. Shell not only accepted the costs of that fact-finding mission but also agreed to pay for development of the new pioneering curriculum which, if successful, would fit so well in the Shell schools of the future.

These ideas were introduced at the Shell headteachers' conference, organised by Fieldwork and Stichting NOB, which was quite an event. With few exceptions the British headteachers, more so than the Dutch, were upset and negative about a move from the English state school system towards a more international system, and the prospect – further in the future – of Shell schools moving from having both Dutch and English streams to having just one, international, stream. Everything was now in the open, and the charismatic and energetic Martin Skelton took the lead in developing the factual subjects for this new curriculum for Shell schools – what later became known as the International Primary Curriculum: the IPC. The role of SNOB in the realisation of the IPC should not be underestimated: Martin Uunk, an educationalist working for SNOB, made a significant contribution. He managed to convince the Dutch Shell teachers that the IPC was a challenge rather than a threat, and he also contributed significantly to the more philosophical aspects of the curriculum.

It took Fieldwork more than four years to develop the dream of providing a cross-curricular and thematic programme for Shell children of all abilities, with more than 70 units of work, spread over three mileposts and based around themes of real interest to the children. I vividly remember, on a visit to the Shell school in Bintulu (Malaysia) during the IPC trial period, how the children – and parents – enjoyed the Olympics, one of the first units of work Fieldwork developed and trialled in the Shell schools. In this small school, the English and Dutch streams were working together under the inspiring leadership of Dutch headmaster Chris Vis, one of the first and most enthusiastic IPC converts, who worked very hard to make the new way of learning a success. It even had a very positive effect on community life in Bintulu because of the involvement of parents in the new curriculum.

For Dutch teachers, the new way of teaching was fundamentally different from what was then common practice in Dutch schools. Traditionally, the Dutch curriculum was taught through textbooks; one textbook per year for each subject. The challenge for the teacher was to present the teaching content in an attractive way and to make sure that by the end of the school year the textbook for every subject was finished. In the IPC, every activity (unit of work) starts with a fact-finding introduction: what do the children know already, what do they want to learn and how will that be organised? The role of the teacher is completely different: it is no longer based on following textbooks and it can be different with every new unit – which makes it more attractive for the children and much more challenging for the teachers! It must be said that it took a while and a few (early) retirements of headteachers before the IPC could be implemented in the Shell schools. It was during this period that the education departments of Shell International in London and The Hague were amalgamated, and I became the sole education advisor for Shell International.

Beyond the Shell schools

It did not take long for Fieldwork to realise that a successful IPC would not only be good for the Shell schools, but would also have potential in other international schools with wide-ranging standards. Martin Skelton made presentations about the IPC at European Council of International Schools (ECIS) and International Baccalaureate (IB) conferences, and at other venues. Wherever he presented, the rooms and halls were packed with an enthusiastic audience and it became clear that the IPC would have potential in international schools worldwide for its focus on academic, personal and international learning. Legally, Shell (as the only sponsor) was the owner of the curriculum, but I realised that the IPC would not develop adequately within a Shell structure. I was also convinced from the outset that this new way of learning would become very popular in other international schools. In the end Shell is an oil company, and developing and marketing a curriculum is not part of its core business.

So Martin and I started discussions about further development of the IPC. In all the years we worked together that was the only time we had a disagreement on the way forward for the IPC. I told him that I flirted with the idea of starting discussions with the International Baccalaureate about the possibility of amalgamating IPC with the IB's Primary Years Programme (which is very much a framework rather than a full curriculum), as in my view the two programmes share essentially the same philosophy. Martin's idea, meanwhile, was for Fieldwork to take over the IPC and to start making it available to non-Shell schools, as well as setting up training programmes for schools that had chosen the IPC. I promised to discuss the question of the IPC's future with Shell International's human resources department. As a result I secured approval for Fieldwork to take over ownership of the IPC, for which Shell in return would have access to all the updates and educational support for the IPC in all Shell schools for an indefinite period of time. In 1998 the agreement was signed, and the IPC went on to become the success story we now recognise: it all started in 14 Shell schools, and that number has now grown to the impressive number of schools and countries in which it is currently offered. Moreover, it has proven itself to meet the needs of specific national curricula, there is a translated version in Dutch (with financial support from Shell International) and a number of Dutch schools in The Netherlands now use the programme.

There is one last note on which this chapter should end: it would not be complete without an expression of my admiration for Martin Skelton. Without him we would not have this wonderful international curriculum: the IPC.

Chapter 2

The IPC: a Shell perspective

Tracey Kelly and Henk van Hout

From the very beginning, Shell's international workforce contributed to its overall success. Testimony to this can be seen in its history books: Shell's first operation in 1892 on the east coast of Sumatra saw a crew of about 400 men, made up of a handful of Americans drillers and refinery workers, European engineers, builders and administrators, Chinese travellers and labourers, Sikhs, and a colourful variety of Indonesian labourers, all dressed in their usual work gear and tensely awaiting the great moment. This arrived on 28 February 1892 when, after almost 10 years of exploration and two more of arduous work to get production under way, crude oil finally flowed from the Royal Dutch wells at Telaga Said (Jonker and van Zanden, 2007). To this day Shell remains a company committed to an internationally diverse workforce and one that, in comparison to its competitors, retains and recruits a high number of expatriates.

The acronym 'IPC' first appeared in Shell vocabulary in the 1930s, when Shell had a 23.75% stake in The Iraq Petroleum Company (IPC). Seventy years later, Shell invested in a completely different kind of IPC which was initially called The Shell International Primary Curriculum, later becoming the International Primary Curriculum (IPC). The IPC was designed to meet the demands of 21st century learning and to be suitable for the diverse cohorts of international children enrolled in Shell schools worldwide. Shell's initial financial and intellectual investment in the IPC, and continued interest in the programme, reinforce the importance of children's education as one of the key factors forming part of what is known in business jargon as the key employee value proposition – the characteristics and appeal of working for an organisation (education, housing, security, medical support and so on) – for Shell and its internationally mobile and diverse workforce.

Shell remains unequivocally committed to providing education scenarios via its international mobility policies. Shell is, however, essentially an energy company with a vision and commitment to be the most innovative and competitive energy company in the world. Its success can be attributed to many general factors such as innovative technology, assets, marketing skills, technical excellence and a clear commitment to providing solutions to a vast range of internationally mobile employees. In order to keep staff mobile, the company offers a suite of additional benefits, one of which is focused on the education of children.

The international mobility of staff is an important aspect in operating Shell companies successfully around the globe. Shell employees with specialist expertise are on international assignments for a defined period (usually four years) in countries where Shell has large oil and gas operations, or has offices to coordinate their regional activities. Such activities are described as either upstream (related to the exploration, production and marketing of oil and natural gas, and including the extraction of bitumen from mined oil sands as well as liquefying natural gas) or downstream (related to turning crude oil into a range of refined products which are moved and marketed around the world for domestic, industrial and transport use, and include gasoline, diesel, heating oil, aviation fuel, marine fuel, lubricants, bitumen, sulphur and liquefied petroleum gas (LPG)).

Employees on an international assignment are referred to as expatriate staff. For Shell's expatriate staff, a special policy team sitting in Shell headquarters in The Hague provides support on all issues around the expatriate employee value proposition, which is all captured under Shell's international mobility policy. The team in The Hague is supported by human resources service centres in Krakow, Kuala Lumpur and Manila which advise staff around the globe in applying global policies on transfer and transaction issues. For expatriate staff the four most important issues, from an employee value proposition point of view, are housing, security, medical provision and schooling for their children. When an expatriate family arrives in a new location, the employee normally hits the ground running, though there is always pressure on the individual, especially those working abroad, because Shell is a very demanding, high-performance company. Children are under pressure as well; depending on their individual situation they are expected to adapt quickly to their new school environment. In their first expatriate posting, they have left behind their national education system where they may have been educated in a different language than the language of the Shell school. In subsequent expatriate postings, when they have previously been educated in an international school in a different host country, they might have to adapt not only to their new school but also to a different curriculum. Nor should the social impact of making new friends and getting used to new teachers and to the new school culture be underestimated. So it is important that such children arrive in welcoming schools with a true international atmosphere of respect for all pupils, parents, staff and others related to the school.

Shell schools

Central to every Shell school is a strong identity driven by the common mission statement, that:

> Shell schools will, through excellent teaching and organisation, maximise children's learning in a way which enables them to achieve high social, personal and academic standards, enjoy learning, adapt to other education systems and develop both a national and an international perspective.

The IPC acts as a vehicle to help teachers to achieve this mission statement and, from its inception, the IPC has become part of Shell schools' identity; not only because of Shell's initial sponsorship of the curriculum, but also because of a firm belief that the IPC embodies concepts that will leverage the best learning for children. The IPC does not advocate a particular textbook, learning activity or pedagogical style, but it does advocate a set of non-negotiable components such as an entry point, knowledge harvest and research and record tasks. This approach was partly influenced by the Dutch approach to education – the Dutch system is driven by 'methods' and places more emphasis on content than was found in other curricula in the mid-1990s. Indeed several features of the IPC were influenced by the Dutch approach: when the IPC was first developed, almost equal numbers of Dutch language and English language streams were found in Shell schools.

Shell teachers

Teachers working in Shell schools are recruited for their proven ability to demonstrate skill and understanding relating to the latest best practice in educational pedagogies. They are expected to promote achievement of the Shell schools' mission statement and to facilitate embracing new ways of learning and working appropriate for the 21st century. This is reflected in the Shell teachers' competency profile, where teachers are expected to deliver technical excellence in various facets of teaching and learning pedagogies. Examples of how this excellence could be facilitated include: having a personal vision and learning philosophy that delivers results; developing interpersonal intelligences that stimulate and achieve effective relationships amongst a culturally-diverse community of children, parents and colleagues; teaching for learning that creates powerful learning experiences, promoting independence and interdependence that help children to achieve a national and international mindset; classroom management techniques that leverage skill development; and continually commit to reflecting and developing professionally.

Twenty-first century learning

Curriculum, pedagogy and the teacher are three factors that strongly impact on learning. Curriculum is at the core of any education system because it defines what schooling should accomplish and specifies criteria in terms of what every child should be learning. The curriculum is paramount in providing the common, coherent and central thrust of what is being taught. Many factors influence children's learning today that were not as prevalent even a decade ago, including globalisation, digital learning and research from neuroscience that can inform education. We are now living in an era where growing numbers of people have access to the internet and technologies, which means that teachers are no longer the key holders of knowledge. These factors have changed the way in which teachers teach and how children learn.

Multi-disciplinary approach

A multi-disciplinary approach is a normal and practised work model within the oil and gas industry, characterised by different sub-teams working towards a common goal which requires multi-skilled teams performing independently and interdependently along the supply chain. Akin to this approach is the design structure of the IPC, which takes a central theme and drives the teaching and learning of knowledge, skills and understanding. The concept of a thematic approach in education is not new; it first appeared in schools in the 1970s and is now back in vogue. The design structure of the IPC has taken this basic concept and modernised it to reflect findings from neuroscientists and the work of other educationalists. For example, an emphasis on how subject disciplines are both independent and interdependent allows children to learn both how things are separate and how they interact. Subject blocks demonstrate the need for 'independent' thinking in a given subject area; tagging subject blocks together allows the student to see the connections between subjects and how they are linked to the big idea, thus providing breadth and depth in each subject discipline.

Defining learning

One of the most influential elements of the IPC, that has transformed teaching and learning practice in Shell schools, is an ability to define learning. The IPC uses neurological perspectives of how the brain works and simplifies this complex field to a simple yet effective definition of learning. This powerful concept and message underpins the ethos of Shell schools as learning-focused schools. The IPC takes findings from neuroscience and marries them to education by describing learning as both a process of consolidating existing learning (familiar information is received and neuronal connections fire faster) and, secondly, as an uncomfortable struggle that takes place when 'new' learning occurs (new things are added and new learning is secured when it is repeatedly practised). This concept of learning has raised the bar in Shell schools as teachers use it consistently to challenge whether learning is both rigorous and appropriate.

Knowledge, skills and understanding

The IPC's learning outcomes are centred on developing knowledge, skills and understanding. Knowledge or information can be gathered quickly from other sources, making the teacher's role one of 'facilitator'. It is important to recognise the value of knowledge as a precursor and building block to developing skills: after all, this is what employees are required to do in the workforce in carrying out due diligence as a precursor to any task. Knowledge is only valuable, however, when it is used to supplement skills and understanding for any task or context. Recognition of this relationship has led to a shift in practice and a re-examination of how teaching time can be optimised in school. For example, the teaching of knowledge can be supported at home (working in partnership with parents), thus providing more curriculum time for teachers to facilitate skill development.

The IPC, when implemented as intended, places greater emphasis on skill development that facilitates the consolidation of 'existing' skills and the learning of 'new' skills. It also uses brain-friendly approaches within activities; for example, it uses a forked approach to tasks (research and record). This approach enables users to synthesise and record their learning, allowing students to demonstrate their skills and understanding in multiple ways through, for instance, multiple intelligences such as logical mathematical or musical intelligence.

The IPC reinforces a lifelong view of learning by viewing the development of understanding as infinite and multi-dimensional. The interplay between knowledge and skills can bring understanding, thus reinforcing a recurring theme of 'interdependency'. More importantly, the IPC uses key questions such as 'What kind of children are we trying to develop, and how can we meet the learning needs of students for the 21st century?' Such questions prompt teachers to reflect constantly on the needs of children in a fast-changing world.

Delivering results

In the past, Shell schools have used surveys to track children and their achievements. Data from these surveys have shown that most children educated in Shell schools are meeting and exceeding the developmental expectations for their age. In 2010, the Shell education department moved away from the Standard Assessment Tests (SATs) used in England to the International Schools' Assessment developed by the Australian Council for Educational Research. These tests are essentially assessing the same attributes as the SATs but do so with a distinct international thread which is deemed more appropriate for our diverse school cohorts. Good results in Shell schools can be attributed to many factors such as small class sizes, extracurricular enrichment, high-quality teaching and the International Primary Curriculum, when it is used as a tool to engage children and support their learning.

International-mindedness

During the 1940s, Shell undertook a series of major harmonizing developments concerning staff regionalisation and internationalisation. Internationalisation was at first the less important of the two, used as it then was with only one very specific meaning: the introduction of expatriate managers (of various nationalities) into a team that had previously consisted exclusively of managers of one nationality (Howarth and Jonker, 2007). The crumbling of colonialism in Asia immediately after the Second World War reinforced awareness that operating companies needed strong local roots if they were to survive and prosper. The overall success of recruiting locally eventually made possible both the Shell Group's rapid post-war expansion and much greater internationalisation; the group was now able to switch key members of staff from one country to another in the interests of wider work experience, the transfer of knowledge and the fostering of a homogenous Shell culture (Howarth and Jonker, 2007).

Diversity and Inclusion and associated programmes are intended to support Shell staff in developing and enhancing relationships with stakeholders both internally and externally. At Shell, diversity incorporates all the ways in which we differ. It includes visible differences such as age, gender, ethnicity and physical appearance, as well as underlying differences such as thought styles, religion, nationality, sexual orientation and education. Inclusion, meanwhile, relates to creating a working culture where differences are valued; where everyone has the opportunity to develop skills and talents consistent with our values and business objectives. The aim is for Shell to be an organisation where people feel involved, respected, connected; where the richness of ideas, backgrounds and perspectives is harnessed to create business value. Diversity and inclusion are clearly interrelated and, to achieve our aspirations, we at Shell must maintain our focus on both. The leading global companies of the 21st century will be those that create a constant stream of innovative goods and services, winning customers and earning loyalty through exceptional performance. No one type of person, or group of people, has all the skills and talents needed, so increasing diversity is not only a good thing, it is rapidly becoming a key competitive factor. Shell, as an established world leader, sees a diverse staff and an inclusive work environment as vital to building relationships.

Shell's diverse workforce and diverse customer base – in terms of race, gender, physical ability and age – are visibly evident. In addition, it has become increasingly important that 'invisible' differences and 'inclusive' practices are also recognised. Seemingly homogeneous workforces, for instance, are in fact different – such as the predominately white Dutch staff working in a refinery in The Netherlands. Inclusion recognises differences and similarities that are largely invisible. Recognising and supporting different ways of working promote the recognition of largely invisible differences and similarities through, for example, working individually, working as part of teams, and valuing the perspectives of others. The IPC promotes a similar philosophy, allowing children to work in different ways – individually, in pairs, in small and large groups – thus giving every child the opportunity to participate and contribute in a range of settings and in different ways, mirroring the real workplace.

The IPC's international goals are given an equal amount of curriculum time to the subject disciplines, which has had a powerful effect on Shell schools: providing a deliberate and planned space to discuss international-mindedness in staff meetings, the classroom and the wider community.

Three personal perspectives
Shell's longest-serving headteacher: Martin Westbury

The IPC is a learning tool. Having worked consecutively in five different Shell schools since 1990, I have seen at firsthand how this tool can be used in different contexts and in different ways. In the beginning I saw the IPC as a massive move forward in terms of the actual content: no longer teaching UK history, for example, to a group of international students of whom many, if not all, had no connection at all to the UK. It can be an exciting learning tool when taught by enthusiastic and talented teachers; it can be a poor tool if used inappropriately. The key message with any curriculum tool or method is to go back to the beginning each time and ensure that learning is the key focus: to ask what is it that we intend the children will learn? In the early days of IPC this was often overlooked; teachers went straight to the activities and some lost focus on what were actually the specific learning intentions. By clearly focusing on learning, teachers can adapt and improve the learning activities to suit both their location and the cohort of children currently in their class.

In my own case, my eldest son moved from Nigeria to China and then to Russia when going from one IPC milepost to another, and this did not cause any difficulties. For my daughter, in moving she was faced with repeating the same unit. She had in any case moved up an age group and the teacher adjusted her learning. I felt that both the revised learning and some consolidation were in fact beneficial to her deeper understanding of the subjects covered.

Having now seen a great many children complete Milepost 3 and move to different international situations, I feel strongly that they have the knowledge, skills and understanding to allow them to flourish. My own son was struck, post-IPC, by how uninteresting some of his new subjects were and how little cooperative learning took place: one downside of moving on from IPC may be that the subsequent learning situation is less fun than before. The other downside for my son was his lack of home country history knowledge. Having some knowledge of the Tudors would have been beneficial to him now that he is in a UK school; whilst he clearly identifies himself as from the UK, he has never lived there. With hindsight, it would have been a good idea to use home holiday leave, as a family, to help develop knowledge and understanding of his home country.

Families new to the IPC need help and guidance in understanding not only the thematic nature of the IPC but also that subject coverage depends on the unit, and that subject learning takes place as a block rather than as a timetabled slot (as may have been the case in another school system). Key challenges from parents along the way have in part depended on different home country comparisons as well as on parents' particular interests and passions. In China, for instance, one parent was an American published scientist: her concern was IPC's apparent lack of science coverage. We subsequently undertook a study of like learning outcomes from schools in the Houston area, USA, and discovered that in fact the intended learning outcomes matched quite closely those of IPC and that, by looking at the route of units we planned, the coverage would be complete if the child stayed with the school through a milepost.

Others miss the traditional subject book and would like to have a book to refer to in order to see more easily what the learning looks like. To compensate, we invite parents into school each term, send a half-term learning newsletter to each class, and at the end of each unit the child's book goes home. The books contain the intended learning outcomes, the children's assessment rubrics both 'for' learning and 'of' learning so that parents can clearly see the child's learning progress, and lots of photographs taken throughout the learning activities. Parents receive a letter explaining the books and are asked to sit with their children who show them what their learning journey has been like through the unit. We ask for parent feedback each time, and this has helped us to develop the process and to include more evidence that can clearly demonstrate the child's learning.

Children who first undertook the IPC during my posting in Nigeria are now at the stage of entering university. Anecdotal evidence suggests that they are doing as well as children from similar schools prior to the introduction of the IPC. It would be interesting to consider whether their university course choices are broader than for previous cohorts, considering the breadth of study undertaken in IPC units. Further anecdotal evidence suggests that some ex-IPC students subsequently chose universities outside their home countries; could this be linked to having developed early international-mindedness?

Current Shell education team: Henk van Hout

Introduction of the IPC in Shell schools at the beginning of this century was revolutionary in terms of 'children's learning'. Children started enjoying learning much more than they did previously. They saw IPC primarily as a subject and when you asked them, 'What is your favourite subject?' the majority would answer 'IPC'!' My own children were very disappointed when they returned to their base country education system in The Netherlands, being educated once again in a more traditional way. Several years after we had returned, they still asked us sometimes, 'When do we get IPC again?' It is now eight years since we repatriated, and recently we asked our children why they enjoyed working with IPC so much. They provided the following answers:

We were working on projects together with children from other classes, not always of the same age. You could learn a lot from each other. We really enjoyed the teamwork. It was an inquiry-based way of learning, very dynamic because we were allowed to walk around, talk about it and investigate as much as we felt we needed to. We could choose in which way we preferred to present the subject, sometimes by putting a play together, or making a work of art or map, so all different ways of working.

The learning did not stop outside the school; we were voluntarily working on it at home, and when you saw one of your peers at the club we would still talk about the project we were working on, or finding a solution for the problem that was presented to us. It was enhancing the collaboration between children of all different kind of backgrounds.

The conclusion of both my teenagers is that children learn better through IPC because they enjoy learning more.

Current Shell education team: Tracey Kelly

One of my most powerful experiences as a teacher was during my assignment at the Shell Ogunu School in Warri, Nigeria, which was an IPC school. On one occasion we took a school trip to Bonny Island, Nigeria. Living in the Delta region, the children were already familiar with an environment where oil and gas operations are very visible. This school trip provided an opportunity to visit the technology centre where the children were able to observe the liquefaction of gas process, and how this process is measured and monitored. This was a fantastic experience which had a significant impact on learning outcomes, especially as we were studying an 'energy' theme – the IPC unit 'Black Gold'. The children were engaged and had a thirst to learn more because the unit was relevant and the IPC encouraged a high degree of practical emphasis.

I particularly enjoyed teaching the international learning goals, and enjoyed exploring ideas and philosophies around what pedagogy looks like for teachers with an 'international mindset'. The IPC offers opportunities to study home and host countries; particularly important for highly transient communities or 'third culture kids'. Further, I was fortunate to have the opportunity to deliver IPC training to teachers working in a range of international schools worldwide. Through this work, I began to see teachers engage in a deeper pedagogical thinking; one that encouraged and consolidated existing good practice and the development of new, innovative and creative practices – for example, a more structured focus to metacognition through the use of the IPC assessment for learning rubrics. This helped teachers to plan children's learning more effectively and to view 'marking' as a tool for learning. The IPC motivated teachers to find out about the multiple ways of viewing 'intelligence'. It encouraged teachers to challenge the most commonly understood and accepted theory of testing intelligence: the Intelligence Quotient or IQ test. The problem with the IQ test is that it assumes intelligence is a fixed phenomenon measurable through one test. The IPC, meanwhile, recognises and endorses the development of a portfolio of intelligences. This change in thinking was quite liberating for teachers but could also be quite challenging, given different cultural and parental expectations.

The IPC also forces a different type of working behaviour for teachers, creating a greater spirit of collaboration. It facilitates greater teamwork between teachers, especially as mileposts fall across different age groups. I found that implementation of the IPC provided an opportunity to re-evaluate whether curriculum, teaching methodologies and intended outcomes are really fit for purpose. The design, structure and underpinning philosophy of the IPC give teachers space and permission to challenge in a collaborative environment.

In conclusion

The decision to introduce IPC into Shell schools was a good one. The concept of comparing the host country to the home country in every unit of work really enhances children's development of an international mindset and formation of a global view on how the world actually works. Learning about other people and their cultures, and learning how to respect others, will make children better global citizens in their future lives. This philosophy is strongly consistent with what Shell as a company expects from its international and national employees. The IPC has demonstrated to Shell that children can successfully switch between education systems such as the International Baccalaureate or the UK, US or other national education systems. IPC encourages children to be more flexible and adaptive, which will contribute to the international mobility of Shell staff. In some traditional 'upstream' countries Shell no longer operates schools. Countries where no international schools existed 50 or 60 years ago can now offer a wide choice of such schools, which means there is no need for Shell to operate a school. Nowadays Shell prefers to work with a school operator or a global education organisation. In such scenarios, where Shell is still heavily investing in international education, IPC has been one of the non-negotiables: Shell schools that were outsourced or divested in the last four years still offer the IPC.

In the remaining Shell schools, we will continue to encourage children's enjoyment of learning through the IPC, in the expectation that they will continue to find it the best preparation for a fast-changing world where adapting skills, understanding and basic knowledge is the key to success.

References

Howarth, S and Jonker, J (2007) Powering the Hydrocarbon Revolution (1939-1973), in *A History of Royal Dutch Shell, Volume 2*. Oxford: Oxford University Press [Published under licence from Boom Publishers, Amsterdam, initiating publishers and publishers of the Dutch edition].

Jonker, J and van Zanden, J L (2007) From Challenger to Joint Industry Leader (1890-1939), in *A History of Royal Dutch Shell, Volume 1*. Oxford: Oxford University Press [Published under licence from Boom Publishers, Amsterdam, initiating publishers and publishers of the Dutch edition].

Chapter 3

The IPC described

Steven Mark

Introduction

This chapter aims, firstly, to set out both the context and key underlying principles that led to the development of the International Primary Curriculum (IPC) and, secondly, to describe the structure of the curriculum. It draws on and uses material available to IPC member schools, which has been adapted here for access by a wider audience.

What kind of world? What kind of children?

Walk into any airport bookstore in any part of the world today and, alongside the shelves of business books and the latest thrillers, we can be pretty sure to find at least one section dedicated to helping us make sense of the world in which we are living. A quick glance at the titles suggests that we inhabit a fast changing world. It is a world that some claim is 'hot, flat and crowded' (Friedman, 2009), or is a 'runaway world [where] globalization is shaping our lives' (Giddens, 2002), where today's children are 'born digital' (Palfrey and Gasser, 2010). Irrespective of the rights and wrongs of individual 'world' perspectives, as a whole they give strong credence to the feeling shared by many: the world for which we are educating our children is very different to the one in which we grew up.

This leads to the first question that any curriculum developer must consider: 'in what kind of world are our children growing up?' It is only once we have articulated a response to this question that we can turn our attention to the next, linked, questions: 'what kinds of children are likely to be successful in this world and how can we help to develop the attributes they will need?' Engaging with these questions is precisely the approach that our team from Fieldwork Education took when they began initial development of the IPC. In formative discussions, the following context was set out of the world in which our children are growing up and in which they will live, and what that means for the kinds of children we are trying to develop:

The muscle economy is going, the knowledge economy is here

Technology is increasingly replacing muscle. Now, it's knowledge, skills and understanding that count. All around the world, jobs go to the people who know and understand what is happening. Knowing things, knowing how to do things and understanding issues are the keys to future success.

We need to be capable of embracing change as well as stability

Just one or two generations ago, a job for life was normal. Now, work and life are very fluid. Increasingly, lives revolve around a portfolio of jobs, a portfolio of places and a portfolio of contexts. Increasingly, 'work' and 'personal' life act on each other.

The idea of 'nationality' is changing

International understanding has become vital. The ability to work with and relate to different cultures is crucial to the new world of work, to our personal lives and to our continuing hopes for a peaceful and sustainable planet.

People need values

Not everything changes, of course. The core values that make people respected, trusted and liked still apply. Values such as honesty, respect, co-operation and caring still matter hugely.

(IPC, 2007)

Beyond these considerations, which argue for the need to help our children to acquire a wide range of academic knowledge, skills and understandings as well as to develop personal dispositions and an international mindset (which IPC and a number of other curriculum organisations term international-mindedness) there is a further key element that curriculum designers must consider. That is the need to help our children to see things and learn things from multiple perspectives. Globalisation, for instance, is a concept that cannot be properly understood purely from an economic or political perspective. We can only make sense of globalisation when we consider it from multiple perspectives: economics and trade, cultural influences, conflict and peace, the political sphere, changing technology and innovation, and so forth. Since 'our experience of the world is cross-curricular; everything which surrounds us in the physical world can be seen and understood from multiple perspectives' (Barnes, 2007: 6), a school curriculum that allows for connections to be made might well offer a platform to demonstrate the kinds of multi-perspectival understanding that the student has (or has not) achieved (Gardner, 2006).

The remainder of this chapter explores how the IPC addresses the need to help children to learn from multiple perspectives. It also details how the IPC articulates the knowledge, skills and understandings that children need to learn across a broad range of subjects (and how this should be achieved), the personal dispositions and qualities that children need to develop, and what international-mindedness looks like in primary-aged children. Specifically, it explores three key structural features of the IPC:

- Learning Goals
- Units of Work
- Assessment for Learning Programme

Together, these three components form the IPC core.

Learning goals

Students no longer ask 'is this what you want?' or 'is this going to be on the test?' Instead, learning goals and standards are clearly spelled out so that students understand them and what they are expected to learn ... know how to demonstrate they have learned it ... and know what to do to improve.

(Wiggins, 1998)

The IPC utilises the core principle articulated here by Wiggins. It takes the approach that curriculum is not just a 'bunch of facts' to be learned in order to pass a test, but that it is rather a means of carefully defining the knowledge, skills and understandings that children need to learn, and using this as a guide for planning all the learning, teaching and assessment that happen within a school. The learning goals are the foundation upon which the IPC is built. They define what children might be expected to know, what they might be able to do, and the understandings they might develop as they move through school. The IPC includes learning goals for:

- every subject of the curriculum
- personal development
- the development of international understanding

Most of the goals have been organised into three groups (or mileposts, as they are described), appropriate for:

- Five to seven-year-olds (Milepost 1)
- Seven to nine-year-olds (Milepost 2)
- Nine to twelve-year-olds (Milepost 3)

These mileposts are among the key organising features of the IPC. One of the main reasons for organising learning across a two or three-year age span – which will be explored in more detail towards the end of this chapter – is that if we want to help children to learn skills as well as knowledge, then we need to recognise that skills take time to learn.

The subject goals

The subject goals cover the knowledge (facts and information children are expected to learn), the skills (practical abilities children need to be able to exhibit) and the understandings (deeper awareness of key concepts which develop over time). There are subject learning goals for:

Art Geography History Information and Communication Technology (ICT) Language Arts	Mathematics Music Physical Education Science Society Technology

Some examples of subject goals are shown in Figure 1.

Language Arts learning goals (Milepost 1)
- Know the names of basic parts of speech
- Be able to recognise and use nouns, verbs, adjectives and adverbs

History learning goals (Milepost 2)
- Know about the main events, dates and characteristics of the past societies they have studied
- Be able to gather information from simple sources
- Understand that the past can be considered in terms of different time periods

Music learning goals (Milepost 3)
- Know how a number of musicians – including some from their home country and the host country – combine musical elements within a structure
- Be able to compose musical pieces combining musical elements within a structure
- Understand that musicians use music to express emotions and experiences

---

Figure 1: Examples of subject goals

The personal goals

The IPC personal goals refer to the individual qualities and dispositions that children will find essential in the 21st century. They define those qualities that will enable children to be at ease with the continually changing context of their lives. There are IPC personal goals for enquiry, resilience, morality, communication, thoughtfulness, cooperation, respect and adaptability. Examples of some of the learning goals for adaptability, for instance, are shown in Figure 2.

Learning goals for **adaptability**: children, through their study of the IPC, will:

- know about a range of views, cultures and traditions
- be able to consider and respect the views, cultures and traditions of other people
- be able to cope with unfamiliar situations
- be able to approach tasks with confidence
- be able to suggest and explore new roles, ideas, and strategies
- be able to move between conventional and more fluid forms of thinking
- be able to be at ease with themselves in a variety of situations

Figure 2: Learning goals for adaptability

The international goals

> Herodotus was aware of man's sedentary nature and realized that to get to know Others you must set off on a journey, go to them, and show a desire to meet them.

(Kapuściński, 2008)

Whilst few primary schools can afford the luxury of sending their children off on an extended Herodotus-type exploration, Kapuściński's observation should give us pause for thought. If we are serious about helping children to develop a mindset that will allow them to think and act globally, then a curriculum that seeks to develop international-mindedness must explicitly and overtly set out what this means, and how it can be achieved in practice by providing children with opportunities to encounter 'the Other'. The IPC has defined learning goals that help young children to begin the move towards an increasingly sophisticated national and international perspective. In essence, this move may be thought of as a journey from 'self' to 'other', or what Gardner (1976, quoted in Wilber, 2001: 18) might call a 'continuing decline in egocentrism'.

The IPC's view of an international perspective is based upon:

- a knowledge and understanding of one's own national culture ('international' is both 'inter' and 'national')
- an awareness and understanding of the independence of, and the interdependence between, peoples
- an awareness and understanding of the independence of, and interdependence between, countries

- an awareness and understanding of the essential similarities between the peoples and countries of the world
- a developing ability to be at ease with others who are different from ourselves

The philosophy of independence and interdependence runs throughout the IPC. It is one of the main reasons for recommending that children's work incorporates both individual and group-based experiences, and for developing themes that encompass a number of subjects but, at the same time, treat subjects individually. Examples of some of the learning goals for international learning are shown in Figure 3 (overleaf).

Milepost 1
- Know about some of the similarities and differences between the lives of children in the different home countries and in the host country
- Be able to respect one another's individuality and independence

Milepost 2
- Know about some of the similarities and differences between the different home countries and between them and the host country
- Be able to identify activities and cultures which are different from but equal to their own

Milepost 3
- Know about similarities and differences between the lives of people in different countries
- Be able to identify ways in which people work together for mutual benefit

---

Figure 3: Examples of learning goals for international learning

Units of work

As explained above, the learning goals (subject, personal and international) are the foundation of the IPC. They set out clearly what children should learn at school: the big concepts and ideas, the qualities we want to help them develop (such as respect and international-mindedness), the key skills and the essential knowledge that will equip them for successful future lives. Though vital, the learning goals only address *what* children should learn and not *how* they should learn. If we want children to learn lots of facts then a traditional, didactic approach may well be effective. But if we also want our children to be independent learners (resilient, cooperative, and so on) then the types of learning experiences they need will have to be very different. This is why the process of learning developed in the IPC (which has taken into account findings from neuroscience and cognitive psychology) allows children to become deep, engaged, active and collaborative learners rather than passive receivers of information.

Like Wiggins and McTighe (2011), the IPC uses the term 'units' for medium-term, detailed plans that set out what and how children will learn over a period of time (such as six weeks, or half a semester). In the IPC these are called the units of work, and there are over 80 of them. Each unit of work is geared around a theme (such as Celebration, or Globalisation, or Structures) that is relevant, engaging and appropriate to children of a certain age range and that offers a rigorous teaching and learning framework. As Wiggins and McTighe (2011) make clear, effective unit planning is not about finding a bunch of activities that are 'engaging and kid friendly ... [but rather about developing units which] ... add up to coherent, focused and generative learning'.

Subjects and themes

Creativity involves thinking outside the box, but you cannot be creative unless you have the box.

(Gardner, 2009)

Before looking in detail at the structure of an IPC unit of work, it is worth considering Gardner's words and what they mean for effective unit design. What Gardner is perhaps in part alluding to – which is fully explored in his book *Five Minds for the Future* where he argues that a disciplined mind, synthesizing mind, creative mind, respectful mind and ethical mind are essential for humans to develop in order to be successful in the 21st century – is that if we want children to be creative, problem-solving, inventive individuals (the creative mind) who can connect learning from multiple perspectives (the synthesizing mind), then as educators we cannot ignore the disciplined mind. In the IPC, the development of the child's disciplined mind takes place in clear subject learning: encompassing not only the learning of a subject's factual content and knowledge but, more importantly, the learning of a subject's skills and thought processes. In essence, children are helped to learn the discipline of a subject, such as learning how to do science and think like scientists (or geographers or artists), for instance, as much as to learn about science *per se*.

The learning of subjects is a key principle of the IPC but, as has already been argued, if we also want children to learn things from multiple perspectives and to make deep connections between these perspectives, then subjects need to be joined together coherently under an overarching theme, thereby allowing children to see the contribution made by individual subjects and how these subjects work together to enhance our understanding of the world.

Structure of a unit of work

The units of work provide practical activities which teachers can use in the classroom, plus a wealth of other supportive information. Each unit is structured to ensure that children's learning experiences are as stimulating as

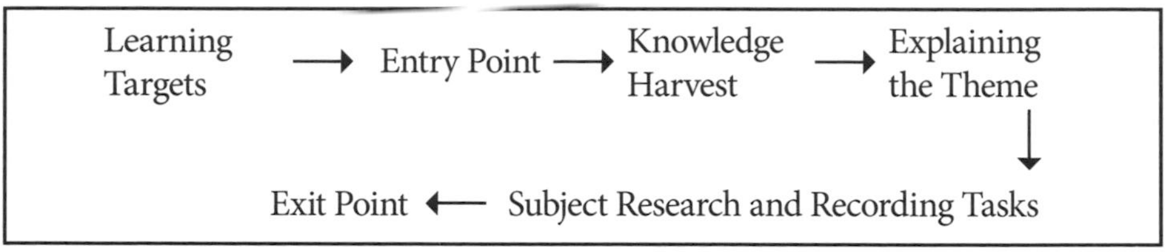

Learning Targets $\longrightarrow$ Entry Point $\longrightarrow$ Knowledge Harvest $\longrightarrow$ Explaining the Theme $\downarrow$

Exit Point $\longleftarrow$ Subject Research and Recording Tasks

possible. All the units follow the same process of learning, as shown in Figure 4.

Figure 4: IPC process of learning for all units

Learning Targets

The units of work are founded on the IPC learning goals – they drive all the learning that takes place in the unit. In each unit of work, the IPC learning goals are expressed as targets. An IPC learning target is a refined learning goal specifically related, where appropriate, to the content of each unit of work.

For example, a Milepost 2 geography learning goal:

'Know how particular localities have been affected by human activities'

becomes targeted in the Young Entrepreneurs unit of work (all about business and enterprise) as:

'Know how particular localities have been affected by money and trade'

The learning targets are firstly defined (for knowledge, skills and understandings) before any IPC units of work are developed.

Entry Point

The entry point is an activity that begins each IPC unit of work and provides an exciting introduction to the work that is to follow. The entry point also provides a common platform so that every child has an experience to draw from in progressing through the unit. Entry points can last from one hour to a week, depending on the age of the children and the appropriateness of the activity. Figure 5 includes an excerpt from the entry point to the Milepost 3 unit of work, Time Tunnel.

Knowledge Harvest

The knowledge harvest is the first formal learning activity in a unit of work. The purpose of the knowledge harvest is to give children an opportunity to share and display what they already know about the theme and the deepening understanding they may already bring with them. The knowledge harvest can be conducted in a variety of ways: through class discussion with the teacher,

Tell the children that, for their entry point, they are going to become designers for a new attraction at a history museum. The owner of the museum wants the children to create a ride called The Time Tunnel, which will take the visitors on a trip through the 'history of the world'. The ride must:

- be suitable for families
- be educational
- feature different periods of history

Divide the class into groups and provide each group with access to books, computers with internet access and art/modelling materials. Each group is responsible for producing a design for their Time Tunnel attraction. They can then present their design ideas to the head of the museum at the end of the session.

Figure 5: Excerpt from the entry point to the Milepost 3 unit of work, Time Tunnel

through discussion between groups of children with feedback to the teacher and class, through knowledge content tests, through simple skills-based activities, and so on. The results of the knowledge harvest can be created as a mind map – either electronically or manually – so that children can see and track their learning as it develops while they move through the unit. The knowledge harvest helps teachers to link new ideas to children's current thinking, to prevent children from engaging in repeated learning that is already consolidated, and to make sure that the activities stay fresh, relevant and appropriate for the children. The knowledge harvest is both a pre-assessment task and a means of allowing teachers and children to monitor their progress as they work through the unit.

Explaining the Theme

This activity involves the teacher helping the children to see the 'big picture' of the unit of work before embarking on the subject learning. It takes place early in the course of the unit and outlines the key questions and tasks that will help to drive the theme at an age-appropriate level. In the IPC theme Time Tunnel, for instance, which focuses on history and chronology, the children explore questions such as:

- How can historical time be recorded and measured?
- How can we sort, sequence and order the past?
- How can we interpret events to explore the attitudes of people in the past?
- How did the movements of people affect the physical and human features of different locations?

It is important that these questions and tasks are articulated and explored at the beginning of a unit (as well as allowing children to formulate their own questions) so that children have a deepening sense of the learning that is possible within the theme. The themes are designed to be rigorous 'learning journeys' and not, as Wiggins and McTighe (2011) point out, 'simply a collection of activities'.

Subject Research and Recording Tasks

Each IPC unit contains a number of research and recording tasks for a range of subjects. Research tasks always precede the recording tasks. The research element of each task is the input part and the recording element is the processing and output part. During research tasks, children use a variety of methods and work in different group sizes to find a range of information. These activities have clearly defined learning targets, drawn from the learning goals. Children engage in an extensive range of recording tasks over the course of a unit. This ensures that they utilise multiple intelligences, allowing them to process and demonstrate their learning using a variety of different cognitive means. Children can, as a result, demonstrate their meaning-making in a number of ways, such as linguistically, mathematically-logically, artistically, musically, or through working with others.

Figure 6 shows an example of a recording task from the Milepost 3 Time Tunnel unit:

In small groups, tell the children that they are going to pretend they are creating their own art documentary for a history channel.

Groups should choose pieces from the different periods they have studied, to talk about as part of their mini-show. Children will need to think about a running order and how they can make thematic links between the art that they have included.

At the end of the session, allow time for groups to present their 'documentaries'. Focus on the choices of art that were made and why they were chosen. Also explore the ordering of the artwork and any thematic links that were made.

[Logical-Mathematical, Visual-Spatial Intelligences]

Figure 6: Example of a recording task from the Milepost 3 Time Tunnel unit

Fundamentally, the IPC tasks (research and record) are designed not as activities as such, but as a means to help children achieve the learning targets. That is why the starting point for every IPC unit of work is, firstly, to identify what we want children to learn and then, as a result, to build a range of tasks to help them to achieve the learning targets. The tasks are practical, hands-on, active experiences. Perhaps the best description of such learning comes from David Perkins (2009), the former director of Harvard's Project Zero, whose book of the same title suggests that we need to 'make learning whole'. Perkins gives the example of children learning to play sport. Often they do so by playing a junior version of the real game – just like children around the world who learn to play football not by playing 11-a-side, full-sized pitch games, but in small versions of the real thing (maybe five-a-side on a small pitch). In essence, children are learning football by being footballers (albeit on a smaller, junior scale). The same is often true for games and hobbies such as chess. Perkins asks why such learning experiences should be confined only to sports or hobbies. This sums up the approach to learning task design in the IPC. If we want children to learn science and geography, to be global citizens and so forth, then the tasks and activities we design need to allow them to think like and behave like (at a junior level) real scientists, geographers and global citizens and not simply to be passive recipients of facts. To achieve this, tasks therefore need to encompass both knowledge *and* skills that can then lead to deeper understandings.

Exit Point

The exit point of the unit of work has two main purposes. Firstly, it helps children to pull together their learning from the unit, allowing them to demonstrate the understandings they have made. Secondly, it celebrates the learning that has taken place. Beyond that, children are encouraged to evaluate their 'learning to learn' skills to reflect on areas such as:

How did they prefer to learn – as an individual/in pairs/small groups/large groups/as a whole class?

What was their preferred style of recording their findings – illustrating/writing/talking/making, *etc*?

This evaluation dimension also supports the development of the personal goals.

Assessment for learning programme
Assessing knowledge, skills and understanding

The nature of assessment is, in part, driven by what it is that is being assessed. Knowledge, for example, can often be assessed effectively (and efficiently) through tests; it requires the recall of facts. Skills, on the other hand, must be assessed practically, as skills refer to what children can do. Understanding is a much more complex issue; it needs to be evaluated over time as it slowly develops, changes and matures. Two different kinds of assessment common to the educational context are 'assessment of learning' and 'assessment for learning'. Assessment of learning is about reporting where children are now ('You can now jump one metre high', for instance). Assessment for learning, meanwhile, is about helping children to learn better ('You can jump one metre, but let's think about what you need to do to be able to jump one metre and ten centimetres'). At different times, both forms of assessment are important: the first (assessment of learning) is about reporting learning, while the second (assessment for learning) is about improving learning.

Amongst the key principles of assessment for learning are the following:

- learning goals and standards should be spelled out clearly
- children should know how to demonstrate what they have learned
- children should know how to improve their own learning
- children should be engaged in the assessment and evaluation of their own learning
- assessment and evaluation should be across the curriculum and not only in a narrow range of subjects

The IPC Assessment for Learning Programme

The IPC has developed a skills-based Assessment for Learning Programme. This is because we believe that skills-learning is at the heart of a 21st century curriculum. That is not to say that the IPC does not value knowledge learning; far from it. Rather, we believe the assessment and evaluation of skills is often where chwildren and teachers need most support, and so an Assessment for Learning Programme provides teachers with a methodology from which to support and assess the development of skills. The IPC Assessment for Learning Programme provides skills-based assessment across eight subjects (art, geography, history, information and communication technology, music, physical education, science, technology) and international-mindedness.

Each of the IPC units of work comprises a number of key skills drawn from the IPC Assessment for Learning Programme. For example, a unit might include the following geography skill for Milepost 3:

Beginning	Developing	Mastering
The child can make simple maps or plans with identifiable features with teacher support.	The child independently produces maps using a variety of scales and symbols.	The child independently produces a variety of maps and plans of different scales.
Some map features may be missing, such as the scale or the key.	The scales and symbols are appropriate to the purposes of the map	The scale is clearly shown and accurate for the purposes of the map
The scale used may not be appropriate to the purposes of the map	The child may need some support with the details of their map or plan. This may involve adjusting the scale, symbols, or the details shown in the key.	The features and symbols shown on the map are all identified in keys which are clearly constructed and sensibly located.

Table 1: Teacher's rubric for geography skill for Milepost 3

'Be able to make plans and maps in a variety of scales using symbols and keys.'

For each of these key skills, clear performance criteria have been articulated in the form of a teacher's and child's rubric. The rubrics detail the performance at three levels, defined as beginning, developing and mastering. For the above geography skill, the teacher's rubric is as shown in Table 1:

The child's rubric is as shown in Table 2.

I'm getting used to it	I'm getting better	I'm really getting it
I can make different maps and plans with my teacher.	I can work on my own to draw maps and plans	I can make maps and plans by myself.
I find it hard to remember the different things to put on my maps and plans.	I use some symbols to show the different places and features and try to put these into a key.	I use symbols and key to show what the symbols mean.
My teacher says I could use different maps and plans to show my ideas more clearly.	My teacher helps me improve my maps.	I draw my maps to the scale shown.
		My teacher says my maps include everything I need to show.

Table 2: Child's rubric for geography skill for Milepost 3

A teacher's rubric and a child's rubric exist for each key skill in each subject, for each milepost. It is not only, however, the subjects that are assessed. Rubrics also exist for the development of international-mindedness and for some of the key personal attributes that feature in subject learning, such as communication skills.

Summary

In summary, the core structure of the IPC has two clear functions: to ensure rigorous subject, personal and international learning, addressed through the learning goals, and to support teachers in their efforts to achieve rigorous learning, addressed through the units of work and the Assessment for Learning Programme. But the IPC also believes that children and teachers should enjoy that learning experience and, at the same time, develop a sense of multiple perspectives, which is why the IPC uses engaging and relevant themes. Learning that is exciting, active and multi-perspectival will, we believe, help teachers to be engaging, inspiring learning facilitators and will encourage children to become lifelong learners.

References

Barnes, J (2007) *Cross-curricular learning 3 -14*. London: Paul Chapman Publishing.

Friedman, T L (2009) *Hot, Flat and Crowded*. London: Penguin.

Gardner, H (2006) *Five Minds for the Future*. Boston, MA: Harvard Business School Press.

Gardner, H (2009) Lecture (as part of the IPC Leadership Conference) given at St Matthew Academy, London on 8 October 2009.

Giddens, A (2002) *Runaway World*. London: Profile.

Kapuściński, R (2008) *Travels with Herodotus*. London: Penguin.

International Primary Curriculum (2007) *Introduction Pack*. London: Fieldwork Education.

Palfrey, J and Gasser, U (2010) *Born Digital: Understanding the First Generation of Digital Natives*. New York: Basic Books.

Perkins, D (2009) *Making Learning Whole*. San Francisco: Jossey Bass.

Wiggins, G (1998) *Educative Assessment: Designing Assessments to Inform and Improve Student Performance*. San Francisco: Jossey Bass.

Wiggins, G and McTighe, J (2011) *The Understanding by Design Guide to Creating High-Quality Units*. Alexandria, VA: ASCD.

Wilber, K (2001) *A Theory of Everything*. Dublin: Gateway.

Part B
The Curriculum Context

Chapter 4

An engaging curriculum: the pedagogy of the IPC

Yolande Muschamp

Introduction

One interesting aspect of the IPC is that its structure extends beyond that of curriculum to incorporate pedagogy through its specification of teaching activities. Additionally, as a curriculum it strives to explain and justify its approach through reference to a range of research – particularly the current findings from research into the working of the brain. This is an unusual combination for curriculum documentation, and models the holistic approach embedded within the curriculum itself. The curriculum, though innovatory, is also located within established traditions of primary education found within the UK, the USA, and increasingly around the world. The IPC has confidently embraced these traditions over the last decade, at a time when many aspects of this heritage have been challenged by national policies for primary education. In this chapter I explore these traditions and the theories which underpin them, in order to examine how they have contributed to the design of the IPC. This analysis allows me to identify the synergies which make the IPC unique and, at the same time, to identify the tensions within the approaches that have created challenges for the future of the curriculum in terms of both review and teaching.

The IPC draws on traditions of primary education through a rich legacy which can be traced back to the influential Plowden Report of 1967 in England (CACE, 1967) and to the work of Dewey writing in the 1900s in the USA. Drawing on these traditions the IPC embeds a child-centred education which has resulted in the development of authentic activities to support the teacher in identifying children's prior knowledge and understanding. This approach also emphasises the importance of capturing children's attention, encouraging children's voice and ensuring their engagement in the shaping and development of lines of enquiry. These four themes (prior knowledge and understanding, capturing attention, voice, and engagement) permeate both the content and methods of the curriculum. I explore these themes and their theoretical pedagogical heritages with particular reference to the entry points of the IPC, and reveal how they create a unique and innovatory combination of pedagogy and curriculum.

In order to explore the traditions and theoretical perspectives that are drawn upon in the IPC and that have clearly influenced its structure and design, I examine the supporting documentation available via the IPC website (IPC, 2012). This includes case studies of practice in schools, lectures and articles by contributors to CPD events, teaching resources, and the curriculum itself. I draw on the guidance for entry and exit points in particular. Within my analysis I use the term pedagogy as it used in the UK and defined by Alexander in his critique of the national policies for education in English primary schools, as:

> ... the act of teaching together with its attendant discourse. It is what one needs to know and the skills one needs to command, in order to make and justify the many different kinds of decisions of which teaching is constituted.

(Alexander, 2004: 11)

Alexander also uses this definition as the basis for his discussion of the long-held view that pedagogy is remarkable by its absence from national polices within England, reflecting the phrase first coined by Brian Simon of 'Why no pedagogy?' – reminding us that Simon was concerned with a view of pedagogy that set out theories of teaching and learning and its discourse which were 'collective, generalisable and open to public scrutiny' (Alexander, 2004: 8). As such the term is a little wider than 'teaching method' – a term often used interchangeably with pedagogy. It is however narrower in definition than that used in continental Europe, which can include all aspects of human development and sometimes even the humanities. My use of the term 'pedagogy' throughout this chapter therefore also relates to the Northern European equivalent term of 'didactics' (Hudson, 2007; Hudson and Meyer, 2011) drawing, for example, on the general and subject didactic tradition of Germany and the scholarly and taught knowledge approaches within the French system of primary schools. Within the IPC, pedagogy is integral to the curriculum documentation and therefore a clear definition of how the term is used becomes unnecessary, other than to say that the guidelines for both teaching approach and curriculum do not extend beyond the field of education and therefore reflect the narrower UK use of the term.

Although without a national affiliation, the IPC does reflect some of the traditions of the national curricula found in the United Kingdom, introduced in the last two decades. The further devolution of constitutional powers to Scotland and Wales may have contributed to the efforts of each country to develop a curriculum differentiated from that of its neighbours. When first introduced, these curricula brought together the traditional primary and secondary phases and presented sequential programmes of study complemented by cross-cutting themes. The curricula contained very little requirement for a particular pedagogy beyond that implicit, for example, in the use of single subjects. At the introduction of the national curriculum to England and Wales in 1989, the articulation of programmes of study through individual subjects was seen as a challenge to cross-curricular planning and did in fact lead to more single subject teaching. Through several iterations, the national curriculum in England has come full circle and a cross-curricular approach to planning is entirely compatible within the framework. This is also the case in Scotland, where the national Curriculum for Excellence has avoided the use of some of the traditional school subjects altogether (for example the reframing of history and geography as social studies), thereby requiring teachers to use a cross-curricular approach. In none of the UK national curricula, however, are teaching methodologies set out in full. Where they have been prescribed, as for example in the teaching of phonics, they remain complementary to the curriculum and are set out within supporting documentation. By integrating pedagogy within the curriculum, the IPC is close to the Scottish curriculum. However the detailed descriptions of the teaching approach, particularly through the entry points, set the IPC apart from all the British national curricula which make no attempt to combine teaching method and content in this way.

Prior knowledge and understanding

The IPC reflects a child-centred philosophy through the selection of content of its curriculum, through its pedagogy and through the international goals set out in the IPC teachers' manual. For example, Milepost 1 states that, by the school year in which children reach seven years of age, the majority of the class are expected to know the home country of each child, understand the cultural differences of the home and respect each other's individuality. Additionally a principle of design of the IPC appears to be to ensure that the entry points to a unit of study provide the opportunity for the teacher to discover the child's current knowledge and understanding. An example of this is the use of mind-mapping in the knowledge harvest at the start of the unit Building a Village, where the guidance states this principle clearly in its opening paragraph: 'in order to find out about the children's existing knowledge and perceptions' (IPC, 2012).

It is this guidance on the identification of a child's current knowledge and understanding, and the suggestions for motivating a child, that genuinely reflect a child-centred approach. This is a significant aspiration. Although the child-centred approach received overwhelming support in England from as early as the 1970s as a result of the Plowden Report, Pollard (1997) showed there was considerable evidence that in practice the use of child-centred approaches was not as widespread as this support would suggest. More recently, in his 2000 international comparison of England, France, India, Russia and the USA, Alexander found a similar lack of child-centred approaches, even in the USA and UK case study schools. Alexander found that it was the case study schools in the USA and England that aspired to the child-centred approach, although he concluded that the aspiration was not met. In the American school he found that:

> The professional discourse of some of the teachers made much of respecting the child's ways of making sense of the world, but having encouraged them to make that sense, they too often left it at that.

(Alexander, 2000: 559)

Of the English case study school, Alexander observed that introduction of the literacy and numeracy hours had disrupted the traditional pattern of organisation of the classroom and resulted in him finding 'a less extreme version of the Michigan condition of children being encouraged to articulate their thinking but lacking a shared vocabulary for doing so' (ibid: 560).

Using Bruner's concept of child as thinker, Alexander placed the identification of children's knowledge and understanding at the centre of teachers' work:

> Seeing children as thinkers ... presupposes that children can and do think for themselves, that it is the task of the teacher to uncover and understand that thinking and through discussion and a 'pedagogy of mutuality' to help the child move from a private to a shared frame of reference.
> (Alexander, 2000: 557)

Alexander's reference to the child's move from 'a private to a shared frame of reference' mirrors the social constructivist account of learning and the work of Vygotsky, a move which is a central task of the teacher. The IPC through its teaching materials clearly models the identification of prior learning as a starting point to each topic and supports the teacher in taking this learning forward. The social constructivist account of learning provides a sound rationale for this view of learning, which I expand on now.

Capturing attention

A significant element of the social constructivist account of learning is the recognition of stages in the learning process where the teacher-pupil interaction acquires a different purpose and requires a different focus. Tharp and Gallimore (1991) explored Vygotsky's ideas and articulated a model to reveal these stages. They suggested that learning occurs in four stages. In stage one a child begins to recognise an activity undertaken by others and is motivated to join in. In stage two the child participates but, as a novice, is supported by more experienced participants in the activity. Vygotsky referred to this phase as a zone of proximal (or 'potential' as Alexander prefers) development (ZPD) where the child's activity and achievement is supported and maximised by a 'more capable other'. The child gradually learns to imitate this support and begins to help her/himself. This process is described as 'scaffolding' by Bruner (1976) and the child takes over control of the activity. As a result the child moves to the third stage where learning becomes internalised and help from the teacher is no longer needed, the child is able to direct the activity and contribute to the future direction of the enquiry. However further challenge or questioning by the teacher creates dis-equilibrium, to use Piaget's term, and leads the child into stage four where learning is discovered by the child to be inadequate or lost, and the child now returns to stage two where assistance from the teacher is again required – albeit at a different level.

The entry points within the IPC are clearly designed to capture the child's attention and therefore reflect stage one of Tharp and Gallimore's model. The topics of the entry points are child-friendly (for example, Chocolate; Inventions and Machines; Time Detectives and Global Swap Shop (IPC, 2012)) and often include a demonstration of skill or activity which reveals to the child a new world or level of expertise in which he/she is invited to participate. Examples of these entry point activities include: a visit to a rainforest or botanical garden, dressing up as pirates, a connections game where children identify their own connection to countries around the world, and a mind-mapping exercise of children's knowledge of other countries through their family connections. The motivation is provided through the enjoyment of the task which is differentiated from routine classroom activity. This enjoyment is then built upon through the development of a line of enquiry or with a challenge to solve a problem.

A return to the work of Dewey, writing some 110 years ago, albeit in a very different context, explains the success of this approach. Dewey (1990) identified 'reflective attention' as a quality of the child-teacher interaction when the child's attention is focused not through interest or curiosity alone, but through a desire to discover something or solve a problem. Dewey demonstrated that successful teaching relied on the creation, development and direction of reflective attention.

Children's voice

A significant dimension of the IPC entry points is the use of everyday activities which encourage children to talk about familiar experiences. The knowledge harvest is a good example of this. An effective case study of the use of the knowledge harvest is provided on the IPC website in the case study republished from *Teach Primary*, which explains how children were asked to look at a world map and identify the countries where they had a family connection. They were then asked to reveal what they knew about that country. As the children's responses were gathered, the teacher then began to organise them under headings determined by the conventions of subject knowledge such as climate and temperature. This restructuring of children's knowledge is an example of the second stage of Tharp and Gallimore's model of learning. A key aspect of this scaffolding is the bridging of the child's own language which is essentially the language of the home, supplemented with the more technical terms of subject disciplines.

This home language or lay vocabulary, representing lay knowledge, is the traditional starting point for activities within the primary classroom and dominates both the content and process of teaching episodes. This approach has long been promoted, as noted by Watts (1980):

> Work generated by language teachers in cross curricular initiatives has been characterised by an 'own words' philosophy: 'children must have opportunities to explore science experiences and science ideas by using their own language – language they understand and use comfortably.'

(in White and Welford, 1988: 5)

Vygotsky (1934/1986) described a lay vocabulary as representative of a lay understanding which is the first stage in a process of transition from natural to mediated forms of cognitive processes. He argued that the school curriculum is the mediated form and comprises a discrete body of knowledge composed of 'scientific' or 'true' concepts which are different from the everyday or lay concepts of the home. He explains learning as the transition from this lay understanding to the mediated form where knowledge is structured by technical concepts. The vocabularies used to describe and explain the lay and scientific concepts may overlap, but words take on new and more specific meaning as they transfer from one to the other. Minick describes the process for the child: 'the child learns word meanings in certain forms of school instruction, not as a means of communication, but as part of a system of knowledge' (Minick, 2005: 45). (Consider how the word 'diet', experienced by children in the home as meaning eating less in order to lose weight, changes in the school science context to refer to an animal's habitual food. A reference to the hamster's diet does not mean the hamster is trying to lose weight.) Minick argues that this is an acceleration of a process that children have begun as they first acquire language.

The transition from a lay to a technical vocabulary will usually involve the correction of erroneous and idiosyncratic understanding of concepts, though this is not always the case. Engeström (2005) makes the point that misconceptions are not necessarily an 'indication of immature thinking. They are culturally produced artefacts which often persist regardless of maturation' (p161), which reminds us that 'the act of naming is not a mental activity but a means of social interaction' (Minick, 2005: 45) and that 'it is essential to keep in mind that the actual and potential levels of development correspond with the intra-mental and inter-mental functioning' (Wertsch and Tulviste, 2005: 63). Transition from the learning that has resulted from this 'inter-mental functioning' for some children will be a radical move to a different way of knowing, while for others it will be an enhancement characterised by progression and continuity.

Although the greater acceptance by educationalists of non-standard forms of language, such as colloquialisms and dialects learned and used in the home, is regarded by many as common sense, this approach has not always been valued and in extreme cases it is seen as a barrier to learning. The debates about standard English, and the introduction of linguistic terms within England's literacy strategy such as 'phoneme' and 'grapheme' to replace 'sound' and 'shape' of letters, are examples of attempts to move away from this philosophy in recent primary policy. In one sense the move to new terms is inevitable and synonymous with learning for both the teacher and the child. Increasingly though, the introduction of a new vocabulary (for example, the recent promotion of 'synthetic' phonics) is used deliberately to challenge and change teaching practice.

Although there is general recognition of the need for a shared language, the primary classroom is not characterised by the purposeful, structured language of instruction (Alexander, 2000). What is more, the promotion of authentic experience of activities for primary aged children, which build on their everyday lives, may even militate against the transition to technical vocabularies. This process of language transition between home and primary classroom is nowhere more sharply observed than in the international classroom where a diverse range of ESL students can be found (Carder, 2011). Within these contexts the vocabulary of curriculum subjects is only one layer in a 'multi-layered world of texts' (Engeström, 2005: 171). The complexity is added to by Gardner's introduction of multiple intelligences (Gardner, 1999) and the different ways of representing knowledge that follow. While the social interaction within the IPC primary classroom remains informal as the entry points attempt to create an atmosphere familiar to the children, it is important to ask if this will in the same way work against the child's development of an understanding of their role within the classroom.

A real challenge therefore for any curriculum, and more especially so for the curriculum of an international classroom, is to provide support for children as they make the transition from home to school. Will children's understanding of the learning process – and therefore their role as a learner – be confused by the expectations raised in the classroom which strives to replicate the familiar conventions of the family home (for example the use of a carpet corner for play or reading stories) rather than emphasise the difference between home and school through a more formal arrangement of furniture? This is particularly significant for the primary phase. Vygotsky's transition will of course have started in the very early years, when understanding concepts will have required children to construct and then separate a concept from an object. Play and imagination are fundamental to this acquisition of concepts. The play philosophy of the early years and the excitement of the entry points within the IPC both continue this process. The entry points successfully bridge the early years philosophy with that of the primary school, which sees a move away from play towards the requirements of the conventions of subjects and disciplines.

Engagement

A development of the social constructivist account of learning, which builds on the ideas inherent in Tharp and Gallimore's model, is made by the community of practice literature, particularly the work of Roth and Lee (2006). This work is of significance to the IPC because of the way in which it extends the account of the learning process by introducing the physical context in which learning activity takes place. Roth's (2003) work focused on taking learning activities out of the school into the community. The IPC entry points do not develop activities in quite this way; nevertheless the authenticity of experience and the real-life contexts promoted within the entry points, and the extent to which they ensure active participation of the child, provide interesting connections with Roth's work.

Roth and Lee identify a community of practice as a shared activity which develops and slowly changes as each participant contributes to the way in which the community works. Pupils, as learners, are new participants in the activities and the domains to which they belong, for example, the subject disciplines or the rules of the classroom. The community encompasses Vygotsky's ZPD, and motivation to join the activity is provided by the shared nature of the activity itself. An example is given of this sharing of experience within the IPC website case study 'A-hoy. Pirates on Board', where teachers as well as children dress as pirates. Roth's projects demonstrate how children's engagement and achievement are much greater when the sharing is extended beyond the classroom and the school to include the local community.

The IPC curriculum does not in itself match Lave and Wenger's (1998) definition of a community of practice, though aspects are evident and provide insight into the efficacy of the entry and exit points which can be seen as small community activities that draw on the children's personal histories and experiences. The activities can be understood as situated within the classroom, where they assume significance and a meaning of their own and reflect Vygotsky's account of the translation of the child's language towards a scientific vocabulary. This situatedness within the primary school is different from the secondary school, but is nevertheless heavily influenced by the specific curriculum subjects of the secondary phase of schooling. Seeing practice within the primary school as activity within a community of practice helps us to appreciate the cultural change required of teachers by the IPC entry points. Roth's (2003) identification of the community through the shared history and practices of its members recognises that a community of practice is dynamic and will evolve and be shaped by the contribution of participants. The entry and exit points although structured within the IPC similarly rely on the participants, the teachers and pupils to share in the shaping and development of activities. This shared experience is significant in ensuring the children's engagement in the learning process.

Conclusion

Despite the rigorous and creative design of the entry and exit points to introduce real-life experiences into the classroom, the challenge remains for the school to ensure the authenticity of the experience. Away from the school, within the community and family context, the communities of practices which children enter respond quickly to a changing world. Updating the subject knowledge, which informs any school curriculum, remains a particular problem for teachers and, inevitably, the pace of change will lag behind changes in the community beyond the school. There are added difficulties for many international schools where there may be little engagement with the future vocational, work-based or training contexts which their pupils will eventually encounter and yet which their curriculum is designed to support.

Added to this is the complexity of mediating different competing cultural and national contexts which all vie to inform the curriculum.

The IPC's solution to the problem of limited or competing domains of subject knowledge is the integrated or topic-based curriculum. This solution draws on the traditional compromise between the real-life experiences of the home and the introduction of pupils to the subject disciplines in anticipation of the conventions of the secondary school. The child-centred approach facilitates and encourages engagement with the community beyond the school gates, encourages a depth of investigation not easily created within a classroom, and addresses contemporary issues of the global context. The entry points provide the opportunity to relate activities to the personal experiences and interests of the teacher and the pupils. The approach also facilitates a differentiation of tasks to match the needs of the individual. The IPC combines topics driven by lines of enquiry, not by a body of knowledge – although the teaching resources provided support teachers through fact sheet and documented perspectives. The collective effort of working this way can be very motivating. Serendipity and obliquity operate alongside planned objectives and focussed activities.

The criticisms and problems which are, however, generated by interdisciplinary topic work are also well documented. A study of Dewey's work alerts us to the possibility that the direction of the line of enquiry, if unsupervised, can be restricted by a clichéd and conservative attitude which fails to provide the dis-equilibrium identified by Piaget as necessary for future learning and progression through the phases identified by Tharp and Gallimore (above). The alternative approach of single subject activities supported by subject textbooks or work sheets and repeated each year, still the traditional diet of many classrooms, promises a safer but less exciting environment for the teacher. The diversity of activity offered by the IPC entry points is very demanding of the teacher's time and effort, and runs the risk of not securing the entitlement that underpins the delivery of the curriculum. This diversity, however, is a manifestation of the 'spontaneous self-organisation' which Jorg *et al* (2007) argue replaces advanced planning, and is a truer reflection of how events unfold in a genuinely unknowable future.

A further challenge within this interdisciplinary approach, and one which must be especially significant for the teacher in an international school, is the discussion of the nature of knowledge itself: how the cultural tensions within what is known, combined with the child's individual personal experience, allow the teacher to assess individual needs. Hopmann's discussion of the concept of Bildung shows the complexity of choice within the curriculum. Hopmann's account of Bildung as an 'unfolding unique individuality' (Hopmann, 2007: 115) adds another layer to the instrumentalism of Dewey's reflective action. Hopmann, by focusing on the impact of the curriculum in terms of a blossoming of an individual, shows how in designing the curriculum, choices have to be made in relation to both matter and meaning when selecting what is core within all domains and in deciding what will support the development of an individual child. Hopmann provides a warning that teaching is not 'one-sided knowledge distribution by the teacher' (p113).

These accounts show how effective learning is likely to be supported by the selection of topics for the units of study to reflect children's interest, combined with the authentic real-life experiences of the entry points. Combined with the rich use of questioning to ensure the teacher understands the children's views and dispositions towards a topic and to reveal the child's understanding, these all combine to deliver an effective curriculum. The processes are socially and culturally determined practices. The four aspects of the IPC highlighted in this chapter – the activities designed to ensure that teachers identify the children's prior knowledge and understanding; the excitement of the entry points designed to capture the children's attention; and the personalisation of the activities which ensure that the children are heard and that they share the shaping of the development of the activities – all promise rich educational experiences. The challenge for the IPC, in the follow-up activities and their related teaching methods, is to avoid the situation which Alexander found in his case study schools where such rich engagement by the child remained at the level of aspiration.

References

Alexander, R (2000) *Culture and Pedagogy*. Oxford: Blackwell Publishers.

Alexander, R (2004) Still no Pedagogy? Principles, pragmatism and compliance in primary education. In *Cambridge Journal of Education* 34 (1) pp7–33.

Bruner, J S (1976) Early social interaction and language acquisition. In H R Schaffer (ed) *Studies in Mother-Infant Interaction*. London: Academic Press.

Carder, M (2011) ESL in international schools and the IBMYP: the elephant under the table. *International Schools Journal*, 31 (1) pp50-58.

Central Advisory Council for Education (CACE) (1967) *Children and Their Primary Schools* (The Plowden Report). London: HMSO.

Dewey, J (1990) *The School and Society, and The Child and the Curriculum*. Chicago: Chicago University Press.

Engeström, Y (2005) *Non scolae sed vitae discimus*: toward overcoming the encapsulation of school learning. In H Daniels (ed) *An Introduction to Vygotsky*. London: Routledge [pp157-176].

Gardner, H (1999) *Intelligence Reframed: Multiple Intelligences for the 21st Century*. New York: Basic Books.

Hopmann, S (2007) Restrained Teaching: the common core of Didaktik. In *European Educational Research Journal*, 6 (2) pp109-124.

Hudson, B (2007) Comparing Different Traditions of Teaching and Learning: what can we learn about teaching and learning? In *European Educational Research Journal*, 6 (2) pp135-146.

Hudson, B and Meyer, M A (eds) (2011) *Beyond Fragmentation: Didactics, Learning and Teaching in Europe*. Opladen & Farmington Hills MI: Barbara Budrich Publishers.

IPC (2012) Available online at www.internationalprimarycurriculum.com. Last accessed 25 May 2012.

Jorg, T, Davis, B and Nickmans, G (2007) Towards a new, complexity science of learning and education. In *Educational Research Review*, 2 (2) pp145-156.

Lave, J and Wenger, E (1998) Legitimate peripheral participation in communities of practice. In R McCormick & C Paechter (eds) *Learning and Knowledge*. London: Paul Chapman.

Minick, N J (2005) The development of Vygotsky's thought: an introduction to Thinking and Speech. In H Daniels (ed) *An Introduction to Vygotsky*. London: Routledge [pp38-58].

Pollard, A (1997) *Reflective Teaching in the Primary School*. London: Cassell.

Roth, W-M (2003) *Contradictions in 'learning communities'*, Keynote paper at European Association for Research on Learning and Instruction (EARLI) Annual Conference, Padova.

Roth, W-M and Lee, Y-J (2006) Contradictions in theorizing and implementing communities in education. *Educational Research Review*, 1 (1) pp27-40.

Tharp, R and Gallimore, R (1991) A Theory of Teaching as Assisted Performance. In P Light, S Sheldon and M Woodhead, *Learning to Think*. London: Routledge.

Vygotsky, L (1986) (original 1934) *Thought and Language*. Cambridge, Mass.: MIT.

Wertsch, J V and Tulviste, P (2005) L S Vygotsky and contemporary developmental psychology. In H Daniels (ed) *An Introduction to Vygotsky*. London: Routledge [pp59-80].

White, J and Welford, G (1988) *The Language of Science*. London: APU/DES.

Chapter 5

International-mindedness and the IPC

Jayne Pletser

Introduction

While participating recently in a course with an international education focus, I encountered a call to arms to international educators; a paper that its author hoped would provoke reflection. It was in this academic context, and away from the hurly-burly of school leadership, that I hoped to find time to reflect deeply on some burning questions. The paper certainly provoked much reflection and addressed a topic that was on my mind. The author of the paper was Terry Haywood, who entitled it 'A Simple Typology of International-Mindedness and its Implications for Education' (Haywood, 2007). The paper challenged the perception that we know what we mean when we talk about international-mindedness. Its aim was to empower schools across the world to reconsider international learning in their own contexts and with each other.

At my then school we had implemented the IPC and, as a team, I felt that we were gently moving along the 'beginning to mastering continuum'. To witness children's enjoyment in their learning, and to encounter the positive attitudes of teachers and parents, was endorsement of our decision to offer the IPC. However, a string of questions continued to remain unanswered, including 'How international is the IPC? How internationally-minded can a curriculum be when there are no generally accepted definitions of international education or the concept of international-mindedness?' and 'How can we educate for international-mindedness at the primary level if, as Skelton (2007) suggests, the prefrontal cortex of the brain, critical to the development of international-mindedness, does not mature until at least 18 years of age?'. I supported the IPC and many of the arguments upon which it is founded, but I still felt that there should be more of a challenge to some of their claims. I decided to use Haywood's typology as a framework to analyse the IPC with regard to international-mindedness. I now invite the reader to consider my arguments, claims and reflections, and to reflect upon your own practice and understanding of international-mindedness.

International-mindedness

Before discussing the analysis undertaken, it is important to consider what international-mindedness might be and how it might be promoted. Haywood argues that the term international-mindedness has sometimes been used generically so that its meaning has been diminished, and he encourages us to think more deeply about that meaning. He argues for identifiable international learning outcomes and believes that there should be many ways of educating for international-mindedness. A one-model approach is not relevant, he feels, though there is common ground for understanding and a greater interaction across cultures, languages and school systems.

Heyward (2002), meanwhile, has argued that international schools with their multicultural populations would be 'better conceptualised as intercultural rather than international' (p10). They should, he argues, actively promote teaching and learning for intercultural literacy – which he defines as the 'understandings, competencies, attitudes, language proficiencies, participation and identities necessary for successful cross-cultural engagement' (p10). The interculturally literate person, according to Heyward, is capable of reading other cultures and flourishing in a cross-cultural setting. The 'multidimensional model for the development of intercultural literacy' developed by Heyward (p16) is a useful model for facilitating a developmental path towards international-mindedness, as it defines the learning features necessary if an individual is to become internationally-minded.

According to Skelton (2007), international-mindedness is located at the very end of the continuum of human development and can be thought of as the 'most complex development of the relationship between "self" and "other"' (p380). Skelton argues that we begin with early egocentric, sensory experiences and move towards the eventual development of independence and interdependence, beginning to accommodate the idea of being a member of a nation, 'and then a part of an inter-nation and then finally independence and interdependence on a global scale' (p380). These descriptions of human development and international-mindedness are consistent with the model of intercultural literacy proposed by Heyward, where the final stage reached is when 'bicultural or transcultural identity is achieved and there is the ability to consciously shift between multiple identities' (p17).

Interpersonal intelligence, according to Skelton, allows a person to 'take on the perspective of the other, creating empathic understandings and working with them, integrating them with their own thoughts and feelings' (2007, pp385-386). Gardner (1993), meanwhile, defines intrapersonal intelligence as when a person has 'a viable and effective model of himself or herself' (p23). These two interpretations suggest that attention to the development of interpersonal and intrapersonal intelligences is critical if the development of international-mindedness is to be supported.

Emotional well-being has a positive effect on the learning process and the development of international-mindedness, while stressful situations and negative emotions can hinder learning. When pupils feel threatened in the classroom, stress chemicals released into the blood stream shut down the neocortex area of the brain, which has a negative effect on the learning process

(Powell and Kusuma-Powell, 2010). It is therefore important that when pupils are moving along the continuum of developing international-mindedness – when they are engaged in what Heyward calls cross-cultural contact, when they are developing relationships with the 'other' – that the curriculum supports and offers opportunities for positive emotional experiences that will enhance the development of international-mindedness.

Skelton (2007) has argued that the design of a primary age curriculum that supports the development of international-mindedness needs to take into account the importance of the brain as an efficient organism, the impact of emotions on learning, arguments about multiple intelligences and evidence about the function and development of the prefrontal cortex (p383). In addition, says Skelton, schools need to develop a culture that deems the 'other' as being profoundly important. Heyward argues that schools need to create the conditions for intercultural literacy if they are to avoid contributing to the development of 'cultural chauvinism and distancing from the host culture' (p19).

From a neurological perspective, it is much harder to unlearn than to learn, which explains why inappropriate learning stays with us. According to Skelton (2007), if early experiences in dealing with the 'other' have been confrontational or difficult, the development of international-mindedness is likely to be problematic. An early start in building positive experiences with the 'other' would therefore seem to be crucial for the development of international-mindedness.

To develop along the international-mindedness continuum and to arrive at a point where one can truly claim to be internationally-minded appears to be challenging, perhaps particularly in the context of a curriculum for young children. Further, as Skelton (2007) points out, neurological research informs us that the part of the brain central to the complex thinking needed for the development of international-mindedness (the prefrontal cortex) does not mature until between the ages of 18 and 23. Why then should we be educating for international-mindedness in primary schools? Bartlett (1998) has argued that the knowledge, skills, habits and attitudes of an international curriculum 'are fostered by exposure to a knowledge base that represents the common ground of human experiences and explores that common ground from a multiplicity of cultural perspectives' (p90); he believes these skills are best developed by starting early. Skelton (2002), meanwhile, has argued that an international primary curriculum and the development of international-mindedness are worthwhile if the learning outcomes and targets of the curriculum take into account pupil capabilities at different stages of their development.

What then are the difficulties faced by national schools when it comes to developing international-mindedness? It could be argued that national classrooms may not have the wealth of cultures in their classrooms that are generally found in international schools. However, there must be very few national classrooms, in any country, that do not have some international connection that can be exploited: perhaps a student born in another country, or with family living out of the home country, or a family member born out of the country. Travel may be another possibility: one does not always have to travel far to encounter the 'other'. Schools may link with schools abroad using technology or engage in student exchanges, or they may consider the objects around them such as clothes, household items and cars. Hill (2000) has argued that a school of many nationalities that does not exploit the surrounding rich cultural diversity can be less international than a national school that takes every opportunity to develop international-mindedness in its pupils and teachers.

Heyward argues that schools need to offer their staff intercultural training if they are to develop intercultural literacy. In a similar vein, Hayden (2002) has argued that teachers in international schools should be role models of international-mindedness, though she fears there is little support for this important aspect of their professional development.

Haywood's typology of international-mindedness

As a response to what he considers a lack of clarity with respect to a definition of the concept, Haywood suggests it is time to identify what the educational objectives should be for an internationally-minded education. In the same way that it is now accepted that intelligence is not a single entity (Gardner, 1996), Haywood argues that international-mindedness is not a sole entity and proposes ten practical forms of international-mindedness (IM) to encourage thinking and reflection so that students may 'develop their own responses and channels of expression' (p85), as follows:

Diplomatic IM	Human Rights IM
Political IM	Pacifist IM
Economic and Commercial IM	Humanitarian IM
Spiritual IM	Environmentalist IM
Multicultural IM	Globalization IM

Diplomacy, according to Haywood, involves a set of core skills and abilities that are essential when considering international-mindedness. These skills and abilities include respect for the country in which the diplomat is operating, along with the ability to learn a new language and its 'verbal and non-verbal expression' (p81). There is an expectation that the diplomat will 'forge constructive ties with the host country' (p81). Political IM differs from diplomatic IM in that it does not adhere to any one national perspective, but may promote the 'best interests of all in global terms' (p81). The skills of political IM are more theoretically based than those of diplomacy and do not necessarily involve the essential diplomatic skills of communication and interpersonal abilities. Haywood claims that trade and commerce have been major contributors to international-mindedness since early times. The necessity to understand other languages, cultures, social and global trends is a must for successful global commerce and these are the skills necessary for the economic and commercial forms of IM. The inclusion of a spiritual form of IM, according to Haywood, derives from the importance of religion to peoples across the world and throughout time, and from the fact that early 'theoretical and ethical bases for internationalism were developed through religious propositions and belief systems' (p82). He points out that 'theologies of coexistence' exist in all of the main religions, and that we must recognise and learn to identify and understand the contribution that religion and religious leaders have made to international-mindedness.

The celebration of 'coexistence' is characterised by multiculturalism and its impacts, says Haywood, lie in the answers that teachers have developed in national school systems with regards to 'teaching concepts, skills and attitudes for intercultural competence' (p83). Arguments for the inclusion of human rights IM, meanwhile, are based around the search for a 'common system of rights applied in all nations' (p83). This is a complex area, and an understanding of cultural approaches and differences is required when considering human rights issues and the search for a common set of rights acceptable and applicable to all. A pacifist IM has been included as Haywood argues that a high value has been placed upon peace throughout our history. As peace is open to negotiation, however, and is dependent upon tolerance, it is necessary to understand pacifist ideology from a diverse variety of cultural perspectives.

According to Haywood, the complicated routes to developing practical responses to humanitarian actions in the face of differing political standpoints originate from a common underlying international-mindedness. It is precisely because of this complex area of developing the practical responses reliant upon international-mindedness that humanitarian IM is included as one of the ten practical forms. In acknowledging that environmental issues have moved away from being local issues to being issues of global importance where solutions demand understandings from many cultural and historical perspectives, Haywood has included an environmentalist IM. He further suggests that environmentalist IM might be part of a wider scientific IM that includes other globally-sensitive issues such as the emergence of new diseases and the impact of biotechnology. The final IM concerns globalisation, which Haywood feels is a 'complex interaction of technological, social, political and economic processes' (p84). The focus of this IM is on the long-term implications of globalisation across cultures and societies.

When adopting a model for international-mindedness, schools are advised by Haywood to take into account their particular context and culture, and to bear in mind that it would be 'imperialist, globalist, and anti-internationalist to presuppose that [the model developed] will also be the most appropriate one for other schools' (p88). Haywood believes, however, that while there should be different ways of educating for international-mindedness, there should be common ground to provide a 'uniform terminology and basis for ongoing enquiry and development by international educators from diverse cultural traditions' (p86). He goes on to identify 'essential' and 'supporting' components as being the common ground for development, where the essential components are as follows.

- Curiosity and interest in the world around us, based on knowledge of the earth and on its human and physical geography
- Open attitudes towards other ways of life and a predisposition to tolerance towards other cultures and their belief systems
- Knowledge and understanding of the scientific basis that identifies the earth's environment as a common entity of value to everyone
- Recognition of the interconnectedness of human affairs (in place and time) as part of the holistic experience of life
- Human values that combine respect for other ways of life with care and concern for the welfare and well-being of people in general

These essential components are the core learning experiences 'that aspire to universality' (p87), while the supporting components – though no less important – supplement the essential components and allow the curriculum to be developed according to the context and culture of the school. The supporting components are as follows.

- The way the curriculum is designed and constructed
- Pedagogy and educational philosophy
- The role of teachers and school organisation
- Approaches and expectations for learning in specific areas not included in the five essential components (including mathematics, the arts and languages)
- Every other aspect of the school

Haywood further argues for the precise identification of formal international learning outcomes in the same way that we set learning outcomes for other subjects in the curriculum. He suggests that learning outcomes, assessment strategies and teaching approaches should be defined by age band.

The International Primary Curriculum (IPC) in action

The design of the IPC takes into account what are argued to be three commonly accepted aspects of the future: that the world is becoming more global, that the muscle economy will be replaced by the knowledge economy, and that a range of jobs will replace a job for life. Each IPC unit consists of an entry point, where the teachers organise an activity that sets the scene and excites the children about the theme. My personal experience suggests that these entry points are much anticipated, and often involve many staff and children from other classes, or they may be organised out of school; the creativity demonstrated here is endless. The knowledge harvest allows teachers to assess what the children already know about the theme. The learning goals present in all units consist of subject goals, personal goals and international goals. The personal goals aim to develop the qualities of enquiry, adaptability, resilience, morality, communication, thoughtfulness, cooperation and respect in the children, while the international learning goals support their development of international-mindedness.

The structure, learning goals and activities offer a developed, systematic curriculum and a framework for teachers that is claimed to develop a sense of international-mindedness in their pupils and themselves. Notions of similarity, independence and interdependence are present, evidence from neurological science has been drawn upon to decide what is appropriate at different ages and stages of development, and learning outcomes and goals take into account the age and capability of the pupils. The development of a culture where the 'other' is of profound importance is a requirement that schools are expected to fulfil.

The structure of the curriculum provides teachers with support for delivering the IPC's international aims, which are to help children learn the knowledge, skills and understanding to become aware of the world around them, to develop the personal skills needed to take an active part in the world, and to develop an international mindset while being aware of their own heritage. The knowledge, skills and understanding required to celebrate diversity and similarity are present in the IPC units. Children are encouraged to develop a pride in their own cultures, which may be especially noticeable in children whose previous experiences pressurised them into being the same as others. I have heard 'international' parents speak of their delight at children's new-found pride in their home cultures and languages. This sharing of home cultures and languages is strengthened by the IPC as children are encouraged to research, with their family, the unit theme from their home country perspective. In today's world of increased technology and communication, it is common for this to include the extended family living 'back home'. Children present findings to their classmates before exploring the themes and topics from the host country perspective. Such an approach is consistent with Heyward's comment that the best cultural resources for developing intercultural literacy in international schools make the most of both the rich cultural mix inside the school and host country knowledge and experiences outside of school.

To ensure quality and to help schools both to define and to improve the quality of the IPC implementation process, IPC has published a self-review protocol, which enables schools to use evidence-based decisions to support their school development (IPC, 2012a). Nine criteria form the basis of the self-review protocol, and the development stages of each of the nine criteria are described at three different levels: beginning, developing and mastering. Schools score themselves on the beginning, developing or mastering scale against each of the nine criteria. One of these criteria is international-mindedness, and one of the basic IPC principles is that schools must implement those elements related to international-mindedness (p11). Schools are encouraged to make explicit the commitment to international-mindedness, and the self-evaluation protocol supports judgements about achieved progress.

An analysis of the IPC in relation to Haywood's typology

In taking Haywood's typology as the basis for an analysis of the IPC and its focus on international-mindedness, the following guiding questions have been asked:

- How does the IPC relate to Haywood's practical forms of IM?
- Are the essential components as outlined by Haywood present in the IPC and, if so, in what ways?
- Are the supporting components as outlined by Haywood present in the IPC and, if so, in what ways?
- Is the IPC internationally-minded according to Haywood's typology?

The following sections will discuss each of the above questions in turn.

How does the IPC relate to Haywood's practical forms of IM?

To answer this first question I looked for similarities between IPC subject learning goals in the units written for older pupils (Milepost 3) and Haywood's ten practical forms of IM. I used the Milepost 3 learning goals as I expected there would be a greater correspondence between the learning goals and IM forms in units written for the older pupils. A table was created (see Table 1) where 'X' denotes learning goals corresponding to Haywood's practical forms. It must be noted that the IPC continues to develop its bank of units of work (IPC, 2012b) and the units included in Table 1 are those available at the time of writing. Referring to Table 1, it is evident that that there was much coincidence between IPC learning goals and the political, economic/commercial, multicultural, environmentalist and globalist forms of IM. There was less coincidence between the IPC learning goals and the diplomatic, spiritual, human rights, pacifist and humanitarian forms of IM. These latter forms of IM are arguably difficult areas of study for primary age pupils, which could explain why the IPC had fewer learning goals in these areas; evidence from neurological science was used to inform IPC developers on age-appropriate learning.

IPC Milepost 3	Haywood's Practical Forms of IM									
Unit themes	D	Po	EC	S	M	HR	Pa	H	E	G
Rulers and governments										
Looking at the evidence		X			X					
Sustainability			X		X				X	X
Settlements			X		X				X	X
Current affairs and the media					X					
Astronomy		X			X					X
Control technology					X					
Host country and home country			X		X				X	X
Making new materials		X			X				X	X
Location (holidays)			X				X			X
The oil industry			X		X			X		
Artists' impressions of the world			X		X				X	X
Health education		X			X					
An historical overview					X					
Energy and fuels										
The big geographical picture					X				X	X
Development					X				X	X
Drug education		X			X				X	
Feelings					X			X		X
The physical world					X					
Investigating rivers								X	X	X
Migration		X			X				X	
Myths, legends and beliefs		X	X		X	X		X		
Sex and relationships education				X	X					X
Trading					X					
Weather and climate			X		X	X			X	X
How we learn		X	X		X				X	
Living things and space environments										
Water		X	X		X				X	X
The Olympics	X				X				X	

Table 1: Subject learning goals in each of the unit themes corresponding to Haywood's (2007) practical forms (x indicates correspondence between learning goals and practical forms)

Key: D: diplomatic; Po: political; EC: economic/commercial; S: spiritual; M: multicultural; HR: human rights; Pa: pacifist; H: humanitarian; E: environmentalist; G: globalisation

IPC personal goals

Development of the personal qualities of enquiry, adaptability, resilience, morality, communication, thoughtfulness, cooperation and respect is supported by the presence of personal goals in each of the qualities (see Table 2). IPC personal goals are not age-specific, but apply across all mileposts (and to adults): they are largely a summary of the personal outcomes of children's learning throughout the IPC and, it is advised, in all other aspects of school life.

Children should be taught in such a way that they develop the personal qualities of:	Enquiry Adaptability Resilience Morality Communication Thoughtfulness Cooperation Respect
Enquiry The vast majority of children will, through their study of the International Primary Curriculum: 1 be able to ask and consider searching questions related to the area of study 2 be able to plan and carry out investigations related to these questions 3 be able to collect reliable evidence from their investigations 4 be able to use the evidence to draw sustainable conclusions 5 be able to relate the conclusions to wider issues	**Adaptability** The vast majority of children will, through their study of the International Primary Curriculum: 1 know about a range of views, cultures and traditions 2 be able to consider and respect the views, cultures and traditions of other people 3 be able to cope with unfamiliar situations 4 be able to approach tasks with confidence 5 be able to suggest and explore new roles, ideas, and strategies 6 be able to move between conventional and more fluid forms of thinking 7 be able to be at ease with themselves in a variety of situations
Resilience The vast majority of children will, through their study of the International Primary Curriculum: 1 be able to stick with a task until it is completed 2 be able to cope with the disappointment they face when they are not successful in their activities 3 be able to try again when they are not successful in their activities	**Morality** The vast majority of children will, through their study of the International Primary Curriculum: 1 know about the moral issues associated with the subjects they study 2 know about and respect alternative moral standpoints 3 be able to develop their own moral standpoints 4 be able to act on their own moral standpoints 5 be able to explain reasons for their actions

Communication	Thoughtfulness
The vast majority of children will, through their study of the International Primary Curriculum: 1 be able to make their meaning plain using appropriate verbal and non-verbal forms 2 be able to use a variety of tools and technologies to aid their communication 3 be able to communicate in more than one spoken language 4 be able to communicate in a range of different contexts and with a range of different audiences	The vast majority of children will, through their study of the International Primary Curriculum: 1 be able to identify and consider issues raised in their studies 2 be able to use a range of thinking skills in solving problems 3 be able to consider and respect alternative points of view 4 be able to draw conclusions and develop their own reasoned point of view 5 be able to reflect on what they have learned and its implications for their own lives and the lives of other people 6 be able to identify their own strengths and weaknesses 7 be able to identify and act on ways of developing their strengths and overcoming their weaknesses
Cooperation	**Respect**
The vast majority of children will, through their study of the International Primary Curriculum: 1 understand that different people have different roles to play in groups 2 be able to adopt different roles dependent on the needs of the group and on the activity 3 be able to work alongside and in cooperation with others to undertake activities and achieve targets	The vast majority of children will, through their study of the International Primary Curriculum: 1 know about the varying needs of other people, other living things and the environment 2 be able to show respect for the needs of other people, other living things and the environment 3 be able to act in accordance with the needs of other people, other living things and the environment

Table 2: IPC personal goals

Consideration of the qualities and their personal goals in Table 2, in conjunction with Haywood's ten practical forms, leads me to argue that an individual developing these personal qualities according to the IPC personal goals could also be considered to be developing international-mindedness according to Haywood's ten forms. The personal qualities reflected in enquiry, adaptability, communication, thoughtfulness, cooperation and respect particularly relate, I feel, to those skills argued as being already necessary for the development of diplomatic IM, with resilience and morality relating to the development of human rights IM.

IPC international goals

The international goals are a summary of the international outcomes of pupil learning at the three mileposts, where Milepost 1 has five goals, Milepost 2 has three goals and Milepost 3 has seven goals. International goals are also present in all of the IPC units, and a perusal of those for Milepost 3 (see Table 3) shows many coincidences between them and Haywood's practical IM forms. IPC international goal 3.5, for instance, states that children should 'be able to explain how the lives of people in one country or group are affected by the activities of other countries or groups'. This statement considered in conjunction with the IPC unit theme 'Trading' suggests a predisposition towards the development of the practical forms of Haywood's political, humanitarian, economic/commercial and environmentalist IM.

Haywood states that multicultural IM is characterised by the celebration of coexistence. This coincides strongly with the IPC stated aims of attributes to be developed by children in an international curriculum; knowledge and understanding beyond that related to their own nationality and an understanding of the independence and interdependence of peoples, countries and cultures.

Though I had initially considered Milepost 3 subject learning goals in relation to Haywood's practical forms, the development of diplomatic IM can also be observed in Milepost 1 (four to seven-year-olds) international learning goals, where it is expected that children will 'be able to respect one another's individuality and independence' and 'be able to work with each other where appropriate' (international goals 1.4 and 1.5). In Milepost 2 (seven to nine-year-olds), the international learning goals continue to develop in, for instance, the areas of diplomacy: 'know about some of the similarities and differences between home countries and between them and host countries' (international learning goal 2.1). International learning goal 2.3 expects pupils to develop this sense of diplomacy and multiculturalism by being 'able to identify activities and cultures which are different from but equal to their own'. International goal 2.3 ('know about ways in which these similarities and differences affect the lives of people') further develops multicultural IM.

The development of political aspects of international-mindedness can be observed in international goal 3.7 ('understand that there is value both in the similarities and the differences between countries'). International goal 3.5 ('be able to explain how the lives of people in one country or group are affected by the activities of other countries or groups') corresponds to the development of political, humanitarian, and environmentalist IM. International goal 3.6 ('be able to identify ways in which people work together for mutual benefit') lends itself to the development of economic/commercial IM.

An international curriculum should develop in children:
- knowledge and understanding beyond that related to their own nationality
- an understanding of the independence and interdependence of peoples, countries and cultures

It should enable children to:
- adapt to other education systems
- develop both a national and an international perspective

It should include:
- a degree of focus on the host country
- a degree of focus on the home country

These characteristics should be reflected in the whole curriculum and in all other aspects of school life. They are assumed in the subject and personal goals. So the following international goals are, in effect, a summary of the international outcomes of children's learning at the three mileposts.

Milepost 3

By the end of the school year in which they are 12, the vast majority of children will, through their study of the International Primary Curriculum:

3.1 know about the key features related to the lives of people in their home country and, where appropriate, their parents' home countries

3.2 know about the key features related to the lives of people in the host country and/or, where appropriate, other countries in which they have lived

3.3 know about ways in which the lives of people in the countries they have studied affect each other

3.4 know about similarities and differences between the lives of people in different countries

3.5 be able to explain how the lives of people in one country or group are affected by the activities of other countries or groups

3.6 be able to identify ways in which people work together for mutual benefit

3.7 understand that there is value both in the similarities and the differences between different countries

Table 3: IPC international learning goals

Are the essential components as outlined by Haywood present in the IPC and, if so, in what ways?

To answer this second question I considered the aims of the IPC alongside Haywood's essential components. The introduction to each IPC unit states that the IPC has been developed to provide support to teachers so that four main aims can be achieved:

- To help children learn the subject knowledge, skills and understandings they need to become aware of the world around them

IPC Unit Themes	Haywood's Essential Components
Rulers and governments	1. Curiosity and interest in the world around us, based on knowledge of the earth and on its human and physical geography
Looking at the evidence	
Sustainability	2. Open attitudes towards other ways of life and a predisposition to tolerance as regards other cultures and their belief systems
Settlements	
Current affairs and the media	3. Knowledge and understanding of the scientific basis that identifies the earth's environment as a common entity of value to everyone
Astronomy	
Control technology	
Host country and home country	4. Recognition of the interconnectedness of human affairs (in place and time) as part of the holistic experience of life
Making new materials	
Location (holidays)	
The oil industry	5. Human values that combine respect for other ways of life with care and concern for the welfare and well-being of people in general
Artists' impressions of the world	
Health education	
An historical overview	
Energy and fuels	
The big geographical picture	
Development	
Drug education	
Feelings	
The physical world	
Investigating rivers	
Migration	
Myths, legends and beliefs	
Sex and relationships education	
Trading	
Weather and climate	
How we learn	
Living things and space environments	
Water	
The Olympics	

Table 4: IPC unit themes and Haywood's five essential components

- To help children develop the personal skills they need to take an active part in the world throughout their lives
- To help children develop an international mindset alongside their awareness of their own nationality
- To do each of these in ways which take account of up-to-date research into how children learn, and how they can be encouraged to be lifelong learners

I would argue that there is much agreement between these four IPC aims and Haywood's five essential components, with a direct correspondence between the first of Haywood's essential components (curiosity and interest in the world around us, based on knowledge of the earth and on its human and physical geography) and the first of the IPC aims (above). The second IPC aim above corresponds to the second essential component (open attitudes towards other ways of life and a predisposition to tolerance as regards other cultures and their belief systems). The third IPC aim relates to both the second and fourth essential components (recognition of the interconnectedness of human affairs – in place and time – as part of the holistic experience of life). IPC's fourth aim is more closely related to Haywood's supporting components, which encompass pedagogy and school organisation.

Consideration of the IPC unit themes (see Table 4) and the five essential components leads me to suggest that the titles of the unit themes lend themselves to fulfilling the demands of the essential components and the development of international-mindedness according to Haywood.

Are the supporting components as outlined by Haywood present in the IPC and, if so, in what ways?

The supporting components relate to the way in which the curriculum is designed and constructed, the pedagogy and educational philosophy, the role of teachers and school organisation, the approaches and expectations for learning in areas not included in the five essential components, and to every other aspect of the school. To answer this third question I considered the supporting components with reference to the IPC.

The opportunity to develop the IPC with respect to the local and school contexts creates the possibility for schools to offer a relevant curriculum based upon the IPC principles of academic, personal and international learning. National and international specialists (who may be parents) are invited into school to share their work and learning experiences. This makes the learning personal (connected to the children's own lives) and international (linked to the international or local community to which they belong). Not only do primary age children enjoy sharing their experiences and knowledge with others, they are enthusiastic about learning from parents, teachers, and peers and are excited when learning about the 'other'. This approach supports the development of intercultural literacy that, according to Heyward, 'can be seen as a crucial element in the creation of a safe, sustainable, and just global community' (p11).

The IPC self-evaluation instrument is relevant when considering Haywood's supporting components, as it is this instrument that allows the school to evaluate itself and its work towards becoming a school that develops the attribute of international-mindedness. Schools score themselves against each of the nine criteria on a scale of beginning, developing or mastering. At the mastering stage of international-mindedness it would be expected that the school demonstrates a deep commitment to the development of international-mindedness; that all of the stakeholders can articulate the school's definition of international-mindedness; that all classrooms provide practical opportunities for each age group of pupils to both develop and deepen their international-mindedness; that the development of international-mindedness is consistent and central to regular reviews of learning and teaching; and that the school has clearly articulated a process for identifying and resolving conflict between diverse viewpoints (IPC, 2012a). This IPC protocol, and the documentation to support it, firmly places international-mindedness as a central issue for school development. However, school development has to take place in the context of the school and its own culture; there are no hard and fast rules, which is consistent with Haywood's assertion that 'we cannot set standards, benchmarks, expectations as an essential criterion for international-mindedness' (p87).

While there is considerable overlap, resonance and agreement between Haywood's ideas and the IPC, a tension arises when considering the supporting components. The tension relates to the fact that the IPC includes typical western approaches to learning that emphasise developing attitudes, knowledge, concepts, and the skills of research and debate. We should perhaps question if the IPC is therefore appropriate in all cultural settings.

Is the IPC internationally-minded according to Haywood's typology?

According to Haywood's typology, the ten practical forms appear to be well represented in both the philosophy and learning objectives of the IPC. I have argued that the least represented forms (diplomatic and spiritual IM) are those that are difficult to develop in such young children. However, the IPC does present age-appropriate learning targets to help children develop the knowledge, skills and understanding necessary for the development of Haywood's IM forms. The IPC is based upon a western philosophy, an approach that emphasises 'the development of attitudes, knowledge, concepts and skills' (p86) and features research and debate – typically western approaches. Haywood believes that such educational models cannot be expected to be 'accepted uncritically' in all cultural settings. Indeed, many readers will be familiar with the cultural dissonance that takes place when new, non-western pupils enter western-approach international schools, and how such pupils have to develop learning behaviours that could be considered inappropriate and deemed rude or disrespectful in their own cultures. Haywood's argument that a curriculum, including typical western approaches to learning, cannot be assumed appropriate in all cultural settings is highlighted within this area of the support components where the IPC's international-mindedness could be called into question.

My conclusion is that the IPC viewed through the lens of Haywood's typology is an internationally-minded curriculum considered from a western viewpoint. Further work will be needed if IPC is to be judged internationally-minded in all settings.

Summary

The IPC philosophy, curriculum design, learning goals and targets together specifically support the development of international-mindedness in schools. What might the conclusion be, however, if a similar review using Haywood's typology were to be carried out by a non-western researcher, in a non-western school?

The potential for intercultural misunderstanding between teacher and pupils, between pupils, and between teachers and parents is enormous in an international school. How far does the IPC go in supporting teachers in their teaching, and pupils in their learning, in reaching their learning potential in the context of their cultural heritage, value systems and understanding? Would many of us disagree with Munro's (2007) assertion that 'learning is influenced by a range of cultural factors that need to be acknowledged explicitly in classroom practice and organisation' (p125)? Hofstede and Hofstede's (2005) work has involved cross-cultural research in 70 countries over a period of 30 years. Their work has affirmed what many see in the classroom, that there are consequences for the learning situation related to 'differences in values related to power distance, individualism, masculinity, uncertainty avoidance, and long- or short-term orientation' (p332). Can a curriculum reasonably claim to be international when it is based upon western approaches to learning? Research in this area could support the IPC in making possible programme adaptations and recommendations to teachers in order to optimise the learning of children from non-western backgrounds. Such research could offer a deeper understanding of the development of international-mindedness in our schools. Individual teachers in their classrooms could also research and 'explore learning from a range of cultural perspectives and encourage reflective learning and thinking from multinational perspectives' (Munro, 2007:125). Munro acknowledges that learning in the international context is complex and his work offers teachers and schools a tool for 'unpacking' the components of learning in the international context. Munro's learning action model consists of a set of 13 learning actions that have both 'generic and culturally specific aspects' (p119) and he proposes that teachers use the model as a tool to examine how their students approach and use each of the actions in turn.

My questioning of the extent to which the IPC is internationally-minded led me to use a typology proposed by Haywood as a lens through which to consider the IPC. After an exploration of the term international-mindedness and Haywood's typology of international mindedness, I considered four questions that would help to guide an analysis of the IPC in relation to Haywood's typology. My conclusion is that the IPC viewed through the lens of Haywood's typology is an internationally-minded curriculum considered from a western viewpoint, which leads me to recommend that further research be carried out if IPC is to be judged internationally-minded in all educational settings.

These reflections, arguments and judgements are clearly influenced by my own experiences, culture and practice in the field. Others would approach the exercise from their own context and possibly offer different interpretations and understandings. It is precisely this interaction and reflection on ideas that Haywood encouraged in quoting Dewey's (1916) assertion that 'things gain meaning by being used in a shared experience or joint action'.

References

Bartlett, K (1998) International Curricula: More or less important at the primary level? In M Hayden and J Thompson (eds) *International Education: Principles and Practice*. London: Kogan Page.

Dewey, J (1916) *Democracy and Education*. New York: MacMillan.

Gardner, H (1993) *Multiple Intelligences – The Theory in Practice: A Reader*. New York: Basic Books.

Gardner, H (1996) Multiple Intelligences: myths and messages. *International Schools Journal*, XV (2) 8-22.

Hayden, M (2002) International Education: pragmatism and professionalism in supporting teachers. In M Hayden, J Thompson and G Walker (eds) *International Education in Practice; dimensions for national and international schools*. London: Kogan Page.

Haywood, T (2007) A Simple Typology of International-Mindedness and its Implications for Education. In M Hayden, J Levy and J Thompson (eds) *The Sage Handbook of Research in International Education*. London: Sage [pp 79-89].

Heyward, M (2002) From International to Intercultural: Redefining the International School for a Globalized World. *Journal of Research in International Education*, 1 (1) 9-33.

Hill, I (2000) Internationally-minded schools. *International Schools Journal*, XX (1) 24-37.

Hofstede, G and Hofstede, J (2005) *Cultures and Organisations: Software of the Mind*. New York: McGraw-Hill.

International Primary Curriculum (2012a) *Self-Review and Accreditation*. Available online from www.internationalprimarycurriculum.com, Last accessed 12 January 2012.

International Primary Curriculum (2012b) *The Units of Work*. Available online from www.internationalprimarycurriculum.com, Last accessed 12 January 2012.

Powell, W and Kusuma-Powell, O (2010) *Becoming an Emotionally Intelligent Teacher*. Thousand Oaks: Corwin, Sage.

Munro, J (2007) Learning Internationally in a Future Context. In M Hayden, J Levy and J

Thompson (eds) *The Sage Handbook of Research in International Education*. London: Sage [pp 113-127].

Skelton, M (2002) Defining International in an International Curriculum. In M Hayden, J Thompson and G Walker (eds) *International Education in Practice; dimensions for national and international schools*. London: Kogan Page.

Skelton, M (2007) International-Mindedness and the Brain: the Difficulties of 'Becoming'. In M Hayden, J Levy and J Thompson (eds) *The Sage Handbook of Research in International Education*. London: Sage [pp 379-389].

Chapter 6

The IPC: what makes it international?

Barbara Deveney

The purposes of a primary curriculum

In reflecting on the primary school curriculum, I was prompted to think about what lessons stood out from my own early school days. I attended a small school on the edge of a town in England, which shared its grounds with a farm. Forty years later I still have vivid memories of going on nature walks and learning how a fox kills hedgehogs, identifying egg shells that had fallen from nests, and being allowed to climb the old yew trees in the school grounds, making them into swings and time machines. I remember being given a newborn piglet to hold and collecting frog-spawn from the local brook so we could watch tadpoles turn into frogs. Most of these memories are about the discovery of the world around me, finding out how and why things happened the way they did, with my teacher always being on hand to answer questions and to provide explanations. I doubt that these lessons were meticulously planned, that there were specific learning outcomes, or even that any particular curriculum was being followed, but I do know that I have remembered these events vividly despite a considerable passage of time, and that I still have the knowledge that I gained through these experiences.

At this point it would be interesting to reflect on what governments consider the purposes of education to be, and consequently how they wish to support these purposes when drawing up a national curriculum. Stoll and Fink (1996) suggest:

> It is the economic agenda, driven by powerful forces in our societies, which has provided the popular answer to the philosophical question 'what are the purposes of education?'. If one was to accept the logic of corporate elites, the purpose of education is to prepare pupils to adapt to the technological revolution so that they will be more useful to the international corporate world.

Alternatively, Powell (2000: 195) tells us that:

> [Education] has been used differently by different nations during different periods of their history, depending upon the need for national myths and heroes, an articulate electorate, a patriotic army of conscripts, an administrative elite, a contented group of tax paying citizens or (most recently) a competitive economic workforce. Today, governments still view

education as the essential vehicle of economic and social development, one of the few remaining instruments of national policy.

There are countless other opinions as to what a school curriculum should be (with a focus mainly on secondary schools) but, if we acknowledge the above reasons wholly or even partly, it immediately becomes clear that any national curriculum would not travel well outside its own borders. Indeed the national curriculum developed for England and, with minor modification, for Wales was never intended for Scotland or Northern Ireland, despite being labelled (incorrectly) the 'British national curriculum' by many international schools. It is hardly surprising then that its use in international schools around the world could be viewed as – at the very least – misguided or, at worst, evidence of insinuating English imperialism. As Cole *et al* (1997: 53) commented:

> Monocultural [British] education attempts to make everyone 'socially and culturally British'. It is the traditional and most practised form of education in Britain and in many ways has been given a boost by the National Curriculum. The main problem with monocultural education is that it has the tendency to reinforce biological and cultural racism, by implicitly and explicitly championing British colonial history and by exalting the supposed superiority of British cultural institutions and 'the British character'.

It is my belief, not least because of my own early school experiences, that an effective primary school curriculum, for all children, should be less the realisation of a political agenda or the maintenance and perpetuation of a cultural *status quo*, and more the supporting of young children as they attempt to make sense of the world around them, helping them to understand their place in an increasingly interconnected world. However, the suitability of any curriculum becomes a far more complex issue when it is to be used in a multitude of countries worldwide and in culturally diverse classes where children have wide-ranging language skills and educational histories. To complicate matters further, many of the children found in such classrooms are internationally mobile and are likely to attend a number of schools around the world, and in different education systems, before they complete their schooling. The role of an international school in the education process is explained succinctly by Sears (1998: 18) in arguing that 'the aim of international education is to give children access to an education in English without diminishing their respect for their own culture and language(s)'. Sears also defines the role of the teacher in an international school as being 'to deliver a programme of instruction that allows for each child's distinct educational and linguistic profile' (1998: 20). Whatever curriculum model is used, therefore, it is essential that it is culturally relevant to each and every child, as well as being meaningful, stimulating and pertinent to the times in which we live.

The need for an international primary curriculum

The development of a specialist curriculum for international primary schools has a relatively long history. I taught in the Middle East in the 1980s and, as there was no published curriculum available upon which to draw, we were required to develop our own programmes of study in order to meet the needs of our culturally and academically diverse students. This was a time before easy availability of computers, so the main research tools were books, videos and encyclopedias. Teachers had to determine what their students needed to learn and decide how to go about teaching it. Schemes of work were painstakingly drawn up, and the worksheets used to support lessons were written and illustrated by hand. Needless to say, teachers themselves had to spend hours researching the detailed information they needed to create their worksheets and to impart accurate information to their students. As many international school teachers were highly mobile, they found they had to reinvent the curriculum wheel each time they arrived at a new school. Whilst many of these teachers undertook their planning conscientiously, the quality of the curriculum was dependent upon the personal strengths and preferences of the individual teachers working on it and, with a regular turnover of staff, there was a clear lack of continuity in provision. This situation was common in many international schools and was highlighted by Bartlett (1998: 79) who, when reasoning why a recognised international primary school curriculum was essential, stated that:

> ... at any given time of year, there will be a group of primary teachers engaged in the business of writing curriculum. They will probably be tired, and probably working on the curriculum after a day in the classroom. Few, if any, will have any training in curriculum development. Most of them will be confused, many of them frustrated.

Although he was writing specifically about the International Baccalaureate (IB) Primary Years Programme (PYP), Bartlett was making a very strong case more generally for the development of a curriculum which would be tailor-made for international primary schools:

> Skills, habits of mind, attitudes, a common knowledge base – these are not developed in the final two years, or even in the final seven years of a child's life in school ... Crucially, they are developed by starting early. They are developed by many years of contact with important ideas. (1998: 90).

The urgency to produce such a curriculum for international primary schools was mitigated, to some extent, by the introduction of the English national curriculum in 1988. As the national curriculum took hold, more international schools pragmatically started to adopt it, particularly the British international schools which mostly recruited their teaching staff from England. However, in view of the fact that the national curriculum arose from a national political agenda and was developed for schools in England and Wales only, with no intention to provide any multicultural themes, it was increasingly frustrating to find that many international schools allowed their teachers to implement that curriculum without adapting it to the needs of their non-English students; it was an exasperating experience to observe young teachers valiantly attempting to teach Tudors and Stuarts to Arab children, Florence Nightingale and the Crimean War to Thai students, and Viking Invasions to the Vietnamese. Such was the context within which the International Primary Curriculum was launched in 2000.

The IPC in international schools

Given this perspective, it is clear that the principal advantage the IPC instantly had over the national curriculum was that it was written with the clear objective of meeting the needs of highly mobile children attending schools around the world and did not represent the promotion of a particular national viewpoint. I believe this is one of the main reasons why it has been so successful in international schools: it offers a refreshing and most welcome alternative to constant adaptation of the national curriculum to meet the needs of classes full of children for whom it was never intended and who have few, if any, links to England (or Wales).

I taught my first IPC unit six years ago, and discovered very quickly that I was required to involve my students in activities which were uncannily similar to those I had experienced in my own early school days (though the foxes and tadpoles were replaced by crocodiles and catfish). Students and teachers using the IPC are actively encouraged to discover the world around them, to go on those nature walks which I so fondly remember, to take a closer look at the world both in and beyond the school, to ask questions and to seek answers about how things work and what makes them tick. I found that the learning in which my students were engaged was wholly meaningful to them and well within the context of their own experiences; any teachers who have been involved with the Teaching ESL Students in Mainstream Classrooms programme (Unlocking the World, 2012) will immediately appreciate the importance of children learning in context. So in restating my belief that a primary school curriculum should help young children to make sense of the world around them, it has to be said that – on one level – this is what the IPC does, and it does the job very competently. The study units cover a wide range of subjects which are culturally broad, inasmuch as they cover global issues rather than national ones. The choice of study units is surprisingly comprehensive and, having taught a number of them from Mileposts 2 and 3, I have yet to encounter one that the students have not found both interesting and stimulating. In addition, the fact that the IPC offers a reasonably loose framework rather than a highly prescriptive mode of study means that teachers can follow their students on their learning journey, and support them with self-made resources and worksheets. On a personal level, this allows me to draw upon those skills that I developed during my years in the Middle East when we created our own study units and, in this way, I can ensure that my teaching is consistently fresh and appropriate for my students.

If we return to Sears' comments above, it can be seen that the IPC easily ticks her first box of giving 'children access to an education in English without diminishing their respect for their own culture': it allows children to learn through using a curriculum that does not promote any one culture above another. On the contrary, it actively encourages students to look at their home countries and host countries and compare them on a variety of levels by considering similarities and differences. Comparisons are made from a simple but unbiased stance rather than from any specific national viewpoint that might be in danger of taking an 'us and them' position, particularly between developing and developed countries. The underlying stance taken is that no hierarchy of countries or cultures exists and no judgments are demanded.

The structure of the IPC also ticks Sears' other box in offering teachers a curriculum that allows for children's 'distinct educational profiles'. As stated previously, many children in international schools move every two to three years as their parents are transferred to new locations by their employers. Children are therefore educated in an assortment of education systems and in schools which may be delivering an international curriculum or any one of a variety of national curricula. Although the IPC is now being adopted by an increasing number of international schools around the world, there is still little likelihood that such children will be moving between IPC schools, unless a parent works for Shell (in whose schools the IPC is widely used). However, the structure of the IPC lends itself to international schools, where children can arrive at any time during the academic year with an endless variety of educational histories behind them, as the IPC is not spiralled to a great extent and its study units are discrete and require no prior experience. The knowledge harvest and mind-mapping activities at the start of each unit, which are both fundamental and unique to the IPC, allow the teacher to find out exactly what prior knowledge the children have, which in turn leads to the starting point for learning. At this point it is worth mentioning that children without specific knowledge of a particular subject area are, nevertheless, still in a strong position to develop their learning. As Thomas (2000: 26) explains:

> Those who are responsible for schooling have, by and large, not always recognized the crucial importance that a child's previous experience ... is already varied, and often so rich that it can act as a sound basis from which new knowledge and different modes of thinking and problem solving can be initiated and developed.

To sum up, it is safe to say that the IPC offers a very large step forward from the use of the English national curriculum in international schools, as it includes a broad range of cross-cultural study units which lend themselves to young children's interest and enthusiasm. It also meets some general criteria relating to the purpose of international schools and the role of international teachers. That said, is the fact that the IPC can be used internationally sufficient for it to call itself an 'international' curriculum? This is a question worth asking, not least because the IPC is now being offered in increasing numbers of UK state primary schools (IPC, 2012), which do not generally identify with offering 'international education'. These state schools may well be educating culturally diverse students, and may well have more student nationalities within their classrooms than do many international schools, which makes the IPC a suitable and obvious choice of curriculum – but one may question why a state school would adopt a curriculum that is being marketed as 'international'.

The international dimension

The IPC covers many of the subjects that one would expect to find in a broad-based primary curriculum, but it adds two other dimensions: an 'international' component and a set of personal goals. The 'international' component includes tasks that ask children to look beyond their host country and home country borders to see how different countries are interconnected, and also attempts to engage students in dialogue and understanding about living in different countries. It is this wider view, I believe, that gives rise to the classification of the curriculum as 'international'. But does this, in itself, make the curriculum international, or would it be better described as simply having a non-national focus? Is the IPC just a very good example of a primary curriculum that recognises that the world is becoming increasingly globalised and that young children need to know a lot more about the changing world than they did in previous generations?

And there's the rub, because as Fail (2011: 106) states when asking what international school teachers bring to the table in terms of their expectations: 'one needs to pay attention not merely to the curriculum (*ie* is it international enough in terms of its content) but how it is taught and how the students learn.' What the IPC offers is, essentially, a set of well-prepared study units that can be used in schools around the world, either national or international, and any school that pays the money can buy the curriculum. However, unlike the IBPYP, the IPC does not appear to have a coherent philosophy with regards to its choice of customers. While the IPC organisation offers teachers in-depth training on how to optimise the teaching of the curriculum via its unique structure and believes itself to be at the cutting edge of recent brain-based education research, it does not appear to identify directly with the culturally-diverse children for whom the curriculum was supposedly written, and it does not endeavour to develop teachers' awareness of how the cultural behaviours that manifest themselves in classrooms may have a fundamental impact on learning. I believe that this lacuna, or missing link, undermines how 'international' the IPC professes itself to be. Walker (2000) makes a relevant point more generally when he argues that:

Although most international schools can be described as 'multicultural' in terms of their student population and sometimes in terms of their staff, the style of learning that they encourage is overwhelmingly in the tradition of Western liberal humanism. This is further reinforced by the origins and nature of the membership organizations, examination systems and accrediting agencies that have supported the rapid development of international education.

The IPC has been written from an undeniably Western perspective and, accordingly, the brain-based educational research from which the curriculum draws emanates generally from Western academia. Dimmock (2000: 107) advises that:

Cross-cultural differences in learning deserve increased attention, since they signal the pitfalls and dangers of narrow ethnocentric, especially Western, accounts of teaching and learning as though they have universal application. If learning processes are influenced by culture, then important ramifications follow. Western research on effective learning may not apply in entirety to some processes of learning as experienced by, for example, Chinese students.

Carrasquillo and Rodriguez (1996: 54, 55) make a similar point in explaining that teaching culturally diverse students:

requires an awareness of learners' cultural background, knowledge of how culture affects motivation and learning, and the skills necessary to work in close interpersonal situations with students of cultures different from one's own.

Thus it is not only important to provide a non-national, non-biased curriculum which has a global focus; there must also be a more profound understanding, by the teachers using the IPC, of the students they are teaching.

The IPC is becoming a very successful teaching tool, and rightly so, but in this success it is important that we remember the children for whom it was originally developed. The children found in international schools are no longer only the offspring of what might be described as the transnational capitalist class (Sklair, 2001), who would wholeheartedly share the values of a Western liberal humanist education. The children we are now teaching in international school classrooms are more diverse than ever: they may be funded by scholarships from around the world, they may be children of host-country nationals who are investing heavily in their children's future, or children whose parents are from developing countries and have been lucky enough to have experienced an education that allows them to enter the international job market. Sears (1998: 7) describes the character of the parents of such children in noting that 'the high esteem which such families feel for their own culture and language makes the lives of second language children in international schools rather different from those of minority language students in national systems'. These children possess a strong cultural identity and deserve teachers who understand how this may affect both behaviour in the classroom and academic performance.

The IPC personal goals

This leads me to the second of the dimensions mentioned above, namely the IPC personal goals, which are indeed worthy – when viewed from a Western perspective. This, again, is where I believe the IPC's case for being truly international is weakened, because while such goals may well sit comfortably within a Western-style culture, the importance of truth and making correct choices (morality), the ability confidently to articulate opinions (communication) and a relentless search for knowledge (enquiry) are not necessarily regarded as positive characteristics outside the Western world. For example, in collectivist cultures where there is high power distance (Hofstede, 2001) children are not expected to articulate their opinions freely and must show deference to their elders, as Dimmock (2000: 47) points out: 'In collectivist societies, people place group goals above their personal goals; they are brought up to be loyal to, and integrate into, strong cohesive groups, which often include extended families.' Confucian Heritage Cultures (CHC) stress the importance of obedience, loyalty, trustworthiness, modesty, frugality, courtesy and similar character traits (Simpson, 1987). In CHC and Southeast Asian countries, the issue of 'face' permeates all levels of social behaviour, so children do not value risk-taking and are often reluctant to ask questions or offer answers for fear of losing face. In IPC terms, therefore, they would not be regarded as good 'enquirers'. Morality is yet another very complex issue outside Western cultures, where telling the truth is not regarded anywhere near as highly as it is in the West. Thomas (2000: 232) sounds a cautionary note for international educators when he states that:

> when children grow up in a community that has a closely knit culture, they will be exposed to a whole new set of values as they embark on their formal schooling ... there will be a value shift on a daily level for each child, from a cultural context with strong collectivist values, to a context in which individualist values will start to be emphasized. This daily exposure to a value shift will in the long run have marked effects on children's cultural values within their community.

If we are to value the children we teach, there is a moral imperative for us to develop an acute sense of their cultural values.

Conclusion

One of the IPC core values is for children to 'develop a sense of their own nationality and culture at the same time as developing a profound respect for the nationalities and cultures of others'. As already noted, I believe that children who move around the world with parents who possess a strong sense of their national and cultural identities will naturally develop a robust sense of self, but how can they be supported in their learning about their classmates' cultures if their teachers have insufficient knowledge of the cultural backgrounds of the students they teach? Cushner *et al* (1992: 28) remind us that:

Few people ever take a formal course in 'culture'. Few ever learn why they behave the way they do, or why they think many of the things they do. Fewer still ever evaluate the assumptions they make. People, generally, lack the concepts and vocabulary with which to talk about these things. Cultural knowledge, like language, is often taken for granted. It is only when we confront someone with different cultural knowledge, who behaves or thinks differently, that we are reminded that our way of doing things may not be the only way.

It goes without saying that any curriculum is only as good as the teachers who deliver it. In the hands of an experienced and culturally knowledgeable teacher the IPC would address the needs of international students very effectively, but this is not always the reality.

If the IPC is to move forward on these issues, there is a fairly straightforward solution. The IPC organisation offers extensive and well-attended professional development programmes which allow schools that adopt the IPC to ensure their teachers are trained effectively in the use of the curriculum. These programmes are offered to new teachers, post-holders, team-leaders and heads, and are organised both in the UK and internationally. It might be opportune to offer additional workshops on the impact of culture on learning to run alongside existing programmes, either written independently or with external input. In this way, as teachers learn more about the IPC, they will also learn how best to implement it with their diverse learners and will gain an improved understanding of non-Western cultures. As Thomas (2000: 115) confirms:

> It is imperative for teachers who work with different cultural groups to be given every opportunity to develop their knowledge and skills to assist them to understand the nature of cultural diversity, and to expose them to relevant cross-cultural research that may assist their professional development.

References

Bartlett, K (1998) International Curricula: More or Less Important at the Primary Level? In M Hayden and J Thompson (eds) *International Education: Principles and Practice*. London: Kogan Page.

Carrasquillo, A L and Rodriguez, V (1996) *Language Minority Students in the Mainstream Classroom*. Clevedon: Multilingual Matters Ltd.

Cole, M, Hill, D and Shan, S (1997) *Promoting Equality in Primary Schools*. London: Cassell.

Cushner, K, McClelland, A and Safford, P (1992) *Human Diversity in Education – An Integrative Approach*. Hightstown, NJ: McGraw-Hill (Kent State University).

Dimmock, C (2000) *Designing the Learning Centred School: A Cross-Cultural Perspective*. London: Falmer Press.

Fail, H (2011) Teaching and Learning in International Schools. In R Bates (ed) *Schooling Internationally: Globalisation, Internationalisation and the Future for International Schools*. London: Routledge.

Hofstede, G (2001) *Culture's Consequences: Comparing Values, Behaviours, Institutions and Organizations Across Nations* (2nd edition). Thousand Oaks, CA: Sage Publications.

International Primary Curriculum (2012) Accessible online via www.internationalprimarycurriculum.com, Last accessed 12 June 2012.

Powell, W (2000) Professional Development and Reflective Practice. In M Hayden and J Thompson (eds) *International Schools and International Education*. London: Kogan Page.

Sears, C (1998) *Second Language Students in Mainstream Classrooms: A Handbook for Teachers in International Schools*. Clevedon: Multilingual Matters Ltd.

Simpson, M (1987) *Children of the Dragon*. Bradford: Bradford and Ilkley Community College.

Sklair L (2001) *The Transnational Capitalist Class*. Oxford: Blackwell.

Stoll, L and Fink, D (1996) *Changing our Schools*. Buckingham: Open University Press.

Thomas, E (2000) *Culture and Schooling: Building Bridges between Research, Praxis and Professionalism*. Chichester: John Wiley & Sons Ltd.

Unlocking the World (2012) *Teaching ESL Students in Mainstream Classrooms*, Available online at www.unlockingtheworld.com, Last accessed 26 May 2012.

Walker, G (2000) One-way streets of our culture. *International Schools Journal*, XIX, 2, 11-19.

Part C

Teaching and Learning through the IPC

Chapter 7

Pupil motivation in the IPC: teacher and parent perceptions

Joanne Marshall

The context

Motivation is a commonly used term in education. I have often heard colleagues make statements such as 'these kids are just not motivated' or 'I just can't get them interested in …'. I have been known to make similar comments myself. But why is this an issue? Motivation to learn is natural, particularly in younger children – as can be seen in their insatiable curiosity to explore, discover and find out things about the world around them. It is said that motivation to learn can be affected by a number of different elements including home life, parents, other significant adults, peer influences and what is being taught at school (Stipek, 1993).

I have taught in primary schools in the United Kingdom and Saudi Arabia, and used both the national curriculum for England and Wales at Key Stage 2 (KS2) and the International Primary Curriculum (IPC). While teaching in Saudi Arabia, the primary section changed curriculum from an adapted form of the national curriculum to a curriculum based around the IPC. In using the IPC I observed a positive change in my pupils' motivation to learn. Parents also commented on a change in their child's desire to study at home. I wondered if this could be attributed simply to this particular class of children, or if teachers and parents in other schools now implementing the IPC were also experiencing an increase in pupil motivation.

My interest in this issue led to a small-scale study, designed to focus on schools that had changed curriculum from the national curriculum to the IPC or which were incorporating the IPC into their statutory national curriculum provision. The research questions upon which the study was based, all relating to teachers' and parents' perceptions, are as follows:

1. Has pupil motivation for learning improved since schools started using the IPC?

2. Has using the IPC increased pupils' interest in what they are studying?

3. Has there been a change in pupil behaviour since starting to use the IPC?

4. Have pupils' study habits changed since starting to use the IPC?

This chapter will begin by identifying the factors that affect pupil motivation for learning, with a focus on curriculum provision. It will then describe the research approach and methods used in the study. Finally there will be an analysis of the data collected, leading to conclusions that provide answers to the research questions.

Motivation

Most educators agree that motivating learners is one of the critical tasks of teaching. In order to learn, individuals must be cognitively, emotionally, and behaviourally engaged in productive class activities.

(Woolfolk *et al*, 2008: 437)

Woolfolk *et al* (2008) and Jensen (2005) suggest that motivation comes from within an individual (it is intrinsic) and therefore provides individuals with a desire to learn or achieve. Intrinsic motivators could be factors such as interest, enjoyment, need to succeed and social acceptance, but these authors also identify negative factors such as an individual's fear of failure. A person who is intrinsically motivated, they argue, is more likely to keep trying and to complete an activity than someone who is not intrinsically motivated. Pintrich and Schunk (2002: 5) take a different stance, stating that motivation is 'the process whereby goal-directed activity is instigated and sustained'. My own interpretation of the term motivation is succinctly reflected in the statement by Child (2007: 226) that 'motivation consists of an internal process and external incentives which spur us on to satisfy some need'. Motivation can thus be seen as being both internal or intrinsic, and external or extrinsic. I have experienced this in classes where some children do extra work because they want to further their own knowledge or improve themselves, while others need external incentives, encouragement or praise in order to complete the same work.

The term motivation is frequently used in teaching, but is often misinterpreted especially in comments such as 'how can I motivate these kids?'. Gilbert (2002) believes that motivation is often looked at from the wrong perspective and that the 'carrot and stick may work if you want a classroom full of donkeys, but real motivation comes from within' (p1). He argues that what we really need to find out is 'how can I get these kids to motivate themselves?' (p2). Alderman (2004: 10) reiterates this point, suggesting that 'the challenge for teachers is to help students develop the motivational beliefs and learning strategies needed for success'.

I believe that motivation is at the heart of learning and, therefore, of child education. However, in my experience it is not always easy to instil self-motivation in every child when there are 25 to 30 children in a class, and the school or national authorities require a fixed and sometimes narrowly-defined curriculum content to be followed. A recurring theme that teachers identify when considering pupils' motivation to learn is that pupils are often uninterested in what they are learning because the content is not relevant to their interests. If we are to improve pupil motivation in our classrooms, therefore, the content we are teaching (and thus the curriculum) needs to be addressed.

The national curriculum for England and Wales Key Stage 2

The national curriculum was introduced into all state schools in England and Wales following the 1988 Education Reform Act, to be obligatory for all state school pupils of compulsory school age. Among its main aims was the provision of a broad and balanced curriculum, and ensuring common standards across schools in England and Wales. The Schools Curriculum and Assessment Authority (SCAA, 1996: 3) commented that the national curriculum was established 'to provide the maximum educational entitlement for pupils of compulsory school age'. Waterhouse (1993), however, argues that there is a wide difference between providing children with their educational entitlement and 'forcing them to learn facts and information in isolation from the experiences and meanings of their lives' (p 35). I tend to agree with this point.

Barber and Graham (1993), MacGilchrist (1993) and Waterhouse (1993) maintain that, in some ways, the introduction of the national curriculum was a good thing in the sense that it was intended to provide continuity for all state schools, and the children in them, by offering a more structured curriculum and clear lines of progression. It also incorporated an assessment structure, which would allow schools to track and compare pupils' progress with those in other schools. My own educational experience has led me to reflect on the importance of continuity and progression, in that my primary education took place at a time when teachers in England could emphasise areas in which they happened to be interested, and these subjects would be covered in detail to the detriment of others.

Having taught the national curriculum at Key Stage 2 (KS2: ages 7-11) in various schools for over ten years, my view is that it tends to be too prescriptive and focuses on the teaching of knowledge, rather than on the skills required to enable pupils to acquire that knowledge and be able to apply it to different situations. It therefore takes little account of how children learn. There is a vast content to cover, which is often not relevant to pupils. A curriculum content that is not relevant or takes little account of pupils' interests can lead to a lowering of, or lack of, motivation to learn. Oliver (2001) discusses curriculum content as a motivational factor, and states that

> [N]either teachers nor pupils will achieve their full potential within the educational process if they are unable to exercise their creativity and pursue lines of enquiry which are meaningful to them in a particular learning context. (p216)

It could be argued that a good teacher can make even the most boring subjects interesting to children and can, therefore, motivate them. The opposite is also true, however, when interesting content is presented in a way that results in pupil demotivation. 'A curriculum is only as good as those who teach it' according to the Cambridge Primary Review (2009: 10). 'In practice, the National Curriculum has so far lacked true balance and coherence, and one of the main tasks of those who wish to reform it will be to put right its design flaws,' argued Brighouse (1993: 112). That reform has since been undertaken with the Independent Review of the Primary Curriculum (IRPC) led by Sir Jim Rose, the final report of which states that 'the touchstone of an excellent curriculum is that it instils in children a love of learning for its own sake' (IRPC 2009: 9). The so-called 'Rose report' did not suggest abolishing national curriculum subjects, but proposed a more cross-curricular approach, based on the findings of the Office for Standards in Education (OFSTED) and the then Qualifications and Curriculum Authority (QCA), in stating that 'some of the most effective learning occurs when connections are made between subjects' (IRPC 2009: 12). This is exactly the approach adopted by the IPC.

The International Primary Curriculum (IPC)

The principle of the IPC is to focus on a combination of academic, personal and international learning for children worldwide, combined with innovative and exciting ways to learn.

(IPC, 2009)

The IPC uses a thematic, cross-curricular approach, where traditional curriculum subjects are taught through, and linked together in, a theme or topic that is relevant to the children being taught (Marshall, 2009). The theorists Jean Piaget and Lev Vygotsky believed that children learn through building on existing experiences, and that these experiences – and therefore learning – can change, adapt or become consolidated as new ideas and concepts are experienced. Their work helped to develop the theory of constructivism, which over the years has helped to influence and shape teaching styles today. 'A constructivist view of learning,' according to Twomey Fosnot (1996: ix), 'suggests an approach to teaching that gives learners the opportunity for concrete, contextually meaningful experience through which they can search for patterns, raise their own questions, and construct their own models, concepts and strategies'.

In my experience the constructivist view of learning really can impact on the way children learn. Explaining to a class at the start of a topic or lesson what they will be learning allows them to see the bigger picture and to use their own existing knowledge and experiences to construct meaning in relation to the situation or concept. I have successfully used a 'pair and share' approach, where pupils are given the opportunity to discuss with their peers their ideas about a concept or question in order to clarify, build upon or even question their thinking about that concept. This interaction with others is an important facet of the constructivist view. By allowing pupils to discuss ideas and link

new knowledge and skills to their interests and exis[...]
should begin to see 'the bigger picture' and to build on [...]

The IPC uses this philosophy and suggests that childre[...]
can make connections and see 'the bigger picture'. An[...]
the application of the constructivist approach is the Chocorate.
many ways in which links are made within this unit, using the pupils
knowledge about chocolate (taste, wrappers, advertisements and so on) and
linking it to designing, making and advertising chocolate – thus connecting
science, design technology, art and English. The way in which these links are
drawn out theoretically makes it easier for children to make connections between
their learning in different subjects, which can lead to a better understanding and
application of that learning. The concept of making connections is central to
the IPC; the curriculum document provides overviews and teaching themes to
which children can relate in terms of their own life experiences and interests.
Using this documentation, and a wide variety of teaching styles and approaches
(visual, audio and kinaesthetic), to present work so that all children have the
chance to access the information, can help to engage, enthuse and motivate
children.

Teachers also need support and the curriculum is one of the most important
support systems for teachers. IPC documentation suggests that the learning
process should be as enjoyable for teachers as it is for the children being taught
(IPC, 2009). A teacher who is interested in, and motivated by, what they are
teaching is likely to promote an exciting and interesting learning environment
for pupils, which in turn could improve their motivation. Having used IPC, this
is exactly my experience; the varied topics and relevant content motivated me
to plan and present the learning in my class in as many different and exciting
ways as I could. The IPC structure takes the pressure off teacher planning, and
the subject matter being studied is designed to interest and motivate which, in
my experience, can impact on teaching approaches and styles.

The study

I set out to see if teachers and parents in a selection of IPC schools around
the world had experienced the same changes in their children's motivation as
I had since using the IPC. Using a web-based questionnaire seemed the most
efficient way to collect the data required, and I opted to use the internet-based
Survey Monkey programme (2012) to design, distribute and collect the data.
Questionnaires were sent to the headteachers of a number of schools around
the world that were using the IPC as part, or all, of their curriculum provision.
I wanted to collect responses from parents as well as teachers, as crucial
stakeholders in their child's education. I did this by asking headteachers
to approach a maximum of five parents and teachers with an invitation to
complete the questionnaire. Separate, though related, questionnaires were
designed for parents and teachers to ensure that the language used for each

appropriate. Both questionnaires started with five closed questions and ded with one open-ended question, which allowed respondents to add their thoughts and opinions about the impact of the IPC on pupils' motivation. By keeping the questionnaire short and using the Survey Monkey programme I hoped to maximise the response rate.

Headteachers were sent an email containing a covering letter explaining a little about the research and what was required of them, including a hyperlink to the questionnaires. Schools were also contacted by telephone. Through a combination of searching the IPC website listing of schools, support from colleagues in the IPC organisation and contacts made at the annual conference of the European Council of International Schools (ECIS), a total of 17 schools were invited to participate in the research. The questionnaire was piloted by headteachers of three other schools using the IPC. A small number of adjustments followed, after which schools were contacted and the email with the hyperlink sent out.

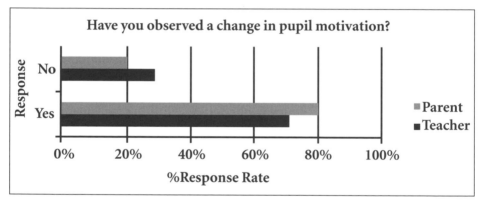

Figure 1: Perceptions of change in pupil motivation

Findings

Of the 17 schools contacted which were then using IPC as part of, or as their entire, curriculum, ten agreed to participate in the research. Responses were received from 39 teachers and 20 parents. Though this is clearly only a very small proportion of the total number of IPC teachers and parents worldwide, this sample has provided some interesting insights. Survey Monkey collates the data and describes it in terms of frequency of responses to each question. Results for the 'closed' questions are presented in the figures below and show the percentage response rate of parents and teachers to each question.

As can be seen in Figure 1, the strength of response to the question about whether pupil motivation had changed was very high. Sixteen out of 20 parents and 25 out of the 39 teachers who participated in this study indicated that they believed pupil motivation had improved at home or in school since the school's

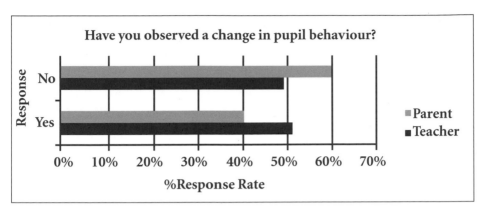

Figure 2: Perceptions of change in pupil behaviour

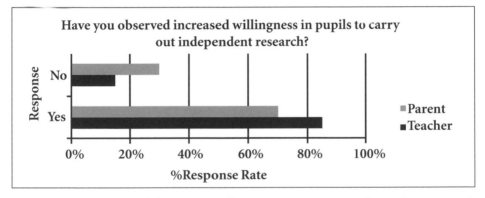

Figure 3: Perceptions of change in willingness to carry out independent research

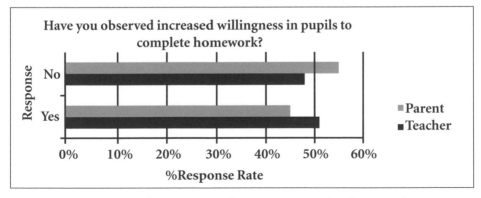

Figure 4: Perceptions of change in willingness to complete homework

introduction of the IPC. We could, therefore, infer that implementation of the IPC, as part or all of the curriculum provision in schools, has resulted in an improvement in pupils' motivation.

What was not included in designing this question was the extent to which, and how, pupil motivation had changed. It should also be acknowledged that there are many factors outside the classroom that can affect a pupil's motivation to learn. Given, though, that these responses are from staff and parents in schools from ten countries worldwide, and that they consistently indicate the same thing, this could suggest that motivation has indeed been improved by providing a curriculum the pupils perceive as relevant.

Woolfolk (2007: 371) states that 'motivation is an internal state that arouses, directs and maintains behaviour'. If this is the case then we might expect that, if teachers and parents had observed improvements in pupil motivation, they might also have observed improvements in pupil behaviour. It is perhaps a little surprising then that only 28 of the 59 parents and staff who answered the question on change in behaviour (see Figure 2) indicated that there was a change in pupils' behaviour, even though 74.5% of parents/teachers perceived that motivation had improved. With hindsight, it would have been helpful to

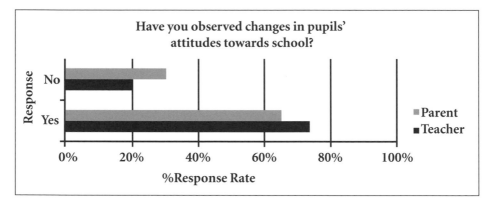

Figure 5: Perceptions of change in pupils' attitude towards school

ask a more detailed set of questions relating to the extent to which behaviour had changed.

Responses to questions about willingness to carry out extra, independent work and to complete homework have been linked together here, as illustrated in Figures 3 and 4 respectively, as they would seem to be related.

When these results are compared it can be seen that, while 47 out of the 59 parents and teachers indicated that there had been a positive change in pupils' willingness to carry out more independent research, only 29 of the 59 parents and teachers felt there had been a change in willingness to complete homework. One possible interpretation of this discrepancy may be that the children do not see the type of homework being set as relevant, though it is impossible to know for sure. QCA (2005: 4) points out that 'the need to make learning relevant to real life' and young people's interests is an important area for improved learner motivation. These findings raise the question, of course, of whether it is the introduction and use of the IPC that has increased pupils' willingness to carry out additional, independent work or whether it is simply that they are being given the opportunity to carry out additional work on subjects that really interest them.

It might have been expected that if pupil motivation had improved, then an improvement in their attitude to school and schoolwork would follow. The results summarised in Figure 5 appear to support this assumption, with 31 out of 39 teachers and 14 out of 20 parents indicating that they felt pupils' attitude to school and schoolwork had improved since being taught using the IPC. It would be interesting, in a larger-scale study, to explore in what ways pupils' attitudes had changed and exactly what had influenced these changes. Was it just the implementation of a new curriculum, or were there other factors (teaching styles or different teachers, for instance) that led to this change in attitude? It would also be interesting, in further research, to ask the children themselves whether they believed their attitude to school and schoolwork had changed and, if so, how and why.

Analysis of the optional, open-ended question

The final, open-ended, question provided qualitative data in the form of thoughts, opinions and feelings about the IPC from parents and teachers: 62.7% of teachers and parents opted to complete it. Responses provided some interesting reflections on the IPC, though not all were directly linked to the original research questions as they also related to perceived problems with the coverage and structure of the IPC, teacher enjoyment/motivation and parental praise for the curriculum. Analysis of these responses will not be included here, as they are peripheral to this study, though they have raised questions which would be interesting to research further at some point. It is interesting that, out of the 37 respondents, only five noted (in each case in a constructive manner) some aspects of the IPC that they believed were not working so well; these points could usefully be investigated further. In contrast, 35 staff and parents responded positively about the IPC, with comments echoing some of the statements made by teachers and educationalists in a number of articles in educational newspapers and magazines.

Responses have been grouped for analysis in the following categories:

- Relevance of the curriculum to pupils
- Improved pupil motivation or enthusiasm
- Improvement in pupils' independent learning and skills

Direct quotes from respondents are included in the following analysis of each category of responses.

Relevance of the curriculum to pupils

Gilbert (2002) suggests that pupils want to have a reason for learning something; it is therefore important that a relevant reason is provided. These points are reinforced in the views of 14 out of 37 parents and teachers who commented that, in some way, the content of the IPC is much more relevant to children today than the national curriculum. Comments from parents and teachers included the following:

'The children enjoy the topics being studied much more now as they seem to relate more to them.'

'It is far more relevant to the children of today.'

'Students are not studying what I consider to be irrelevant material for their age and culture.'

'The IPC is my preferred choice … [it] enables my children to focus on topics relevant to today, how to research and [it] enhances their creativity.'

Not only did most of the teachers and parents who answered this question comment on the relevance of the content of the IPC, they also pointed out that the cross-curricular approach helps children to link their ideas and understanding across subjects:

'The cross-curricular thematic approach makes learning more relevant and … can be more easily applied to real world situations.'

'Children can see links across the subjects that tie things together.'

Although it is true that 14 out of 37 is only a small proportion of those who took part in this study, and an even smaller proportion of the total population of teachers and parents of pupils in IPC schools, a general theme in the responses indicates a perception that the IPC's content is more relevant to children in schools today than that of the national curriculum. Additionally these similar responses arose from a range of schools in ten countries, which indicates some consistency of experience.

Improved pupil motivation or enthusiasm

Clearly the relevance of curriculum content and the improvement in pupils' enthusiasm and motivation are interrelated, as noted by Woolfolk in suggesting that 'students' interest in and excitement about what they are learning is one of the most important factors in education' (2007: 405). Twenty-two of the 37 parents and teachers who responded to this question indicated, in some way, that pupils' motivation or enthusiasm had been enhanced since using the IPC:

'I feel this is a child-centred curriculum and it engages the students' interests. They show a lot more enthusiasm to learn.'

'The children seem to be more motivated and show more enthusiasm toward their learning.'

'I can see a difference in their motivation, enthusiasm and interest.'

What is not clear is *how* pupil motivation has increased, or what has caused it to increase. While it could be argued that the introduction of the IPC has had this effect, other external and internal factors that are nothing to do with school could also have led to this improvement. One possible factor is teacher motivation; it could be argued that use of the IPC affects pupil motivation both directly and indirectly through the attitude of the teachers. Alderman (2004: 274) suggests 'the successful implementation of motivational strategies depends a great deal on the teacher's motivation', a point reiterated in a comment by one teacher respondent who said:

'I love working with the IPC. I find the pupils so motivated ... The IPC sets them on fire! They love it to bits and so do I.'

Having used both the IPC and the national curriculum, my own experience is that implementing the IPC did indeed contribute to an increase in both my own motivation and that of the pupils in my class.

Improvement in pupils' independent learning and skills

Twelve of the 37 parents and teachers who completed this question commented on an improvement in pupils' independent learning and skills. IPC (2001: 6) suggests that the activities children are given at school 'will help them develop their own personal attributes', and letting them work on their own or in small or large groups will help them to 'develop the ability to work independently and interdependently'. Comments including the following suggest there is evidence to support such claims:

'[The IPC] is more enquiry based, so the children have learned to become more independent in their research skills.'

'The children can direct their learning to a certain degree.'

Woolfolk's comment (2007) that children who feel in control of their learning are likely to put more effort into their work, use better strategies and persist longer in schoolwork is supported by two respondents, who made the following observations:

'My child now does her homework and studies by herself without any aid from me, [and] frequently researches a subject by herself because she wants to be informed.'

'I have often had pupils asking if they are 'allowed' to take their IPC books home to do extra research over the weekend – case closed!'

Conclusion

As the findings of this study arise from ten different schools located around the world, it could be inferred that using the IPC in some form, as part of all of a school's curriculum provision, might improve pupil motivation, regardless of context. Parents and teachers perceived that introduction of the IPC had improved pupils' interest in what they were studying and increased their motivation, though participants' perception of whether pupil behaviour had changed was less conclusive. Responses to other questions suggest that introduction of the IPC could have contributed to an overall improvement in pupils' study habits, though they also suggest that willingness to complete homework had not improved as much as willingness to carry out additional, independent research. This latter finding could be linked to the fact that IPC provides topics to be studied that are relevant to most children, which could well stimulate their curiosity to research a subject in more depth.

Overall, the results suggest that improvement in pupils' motivation, interest, study habits and behaviour could be attributed to a school's use of the IPC. This was, however, a small-scale project which only included a very small sample of the entire population of IPC stakeholders worldwide, and it is important in viewing its findings to recognise their limitations; the conclusions must be taken in context and cannot be assumed to apply to every school using the IPC. It is also important to acknowledge that many factors, circumstances and people outside school can influence a pupil's motivation.

Notwithstanding the small scale of the study, and the caution with which its findings must be interpreted, light has been shone on a little-researched area and insight has been provided, albeit in a limited fashion, into the rapidly growing IPC. A modified and larger-scale follow-up to this study would undoubtedly provide further interesting results, as would research on children's perceptions of the IPC, and research with teachers using the IPC in different types of school worldwide. As the IPC grows, the potential for informative and illuminating research into this innovative curriculum will undoubtedly grow with it.

Acknowledgement

I would like to thank the International Primary Curriculum for allowing me access to their website and resources, and the teachers and parents who took the time to respond to the questionnaire. Without their cooperation this study could not have been completed.

References

Alderman, M K (2004) *Motivation for Achievement: Possibilities for Teaching and Learning* (2nd ed). New Jersey: Lawrence Erlbaum Associates Inc.

Anderson, G with Arsenault, N (2007) *Fundamentals of Educational Research* (2nd ed). London: Routledge.

Barber, M and Graham, D (1993) Common Sense: A Programme for the Future, in M Barber and D Graham (eds) *Sense, Nonsense and the National Curriculum*. London: Falmer Press.

Brighouse, T (1993) The Future: Getting beyond Mastermind in the National Curriculum, in M Barber and D Graham (eds) *Sense, Nonsense and the National Curriculum*. London: Falmer Press.

Cambridge Primary Review (2009) *Towards a New Primary Curriculum: a report from the Cambridge Primary Review*. Part 2: The Future. Cambridge: University of Cambridge Faculty of Education.

Child, D (2007) *Psychology and the Teacher*. New York: Continuum International Publishing group.

Gilbert, I (2002) *Essential Motivation in the Classroom*. London: Routledge.

Independent Review of the Primary Curriculum (2009) Final Report: Department for Children, Schools and Families website, www.dcsf.gov.uk (last accessed 10 July 2009).

International Primary Curriculum (2001) Learning Goals and Background Information folder: IPC.

International Primary Curriculum (2012) Available online at www.internationalprimarycurriculum.com (last accessed 8 June 2012).

Jensen, E (2005) *Teaching with the Brain in Mind* (2nd ed). Virginia: Library of Association for Supervision and Curriculum Development.

MacGilchrist, B (1993) A Primary Perspective on the National Curriculum, in P O'Hear and J White (eds) (1993) *Assessing the National Curriculum*. London: Paul Chapman Publishing Ltd.

Marshall, J (2009) Is the International Primary Curriculum a more motivational curriculum than the National Curriculum of England and Wales? University of Bath: Unpublished MA assignment for Understanding Learners and Learning unit.

Oliver, P (2001) Conclusion: Logic, Rationality and the Curriculum, in C Cullingford and P Oliver (ed) (2001) *The National Curriculum and Its Effects*. Aldershot: Ashgate Publishing Ltd.

Pintrich, P R and Schunk D H (2002) *Motivation in Education: Theory, Research and Applications* (2nd ed). Englewood Cliffs, New Jersey: Prentice-Hall.

QCA Futures Research (2005) *Learner Motivation: An International Review*. www.qca.org.uk (last accessed 10 July 2009).

Schools Curriculum and Assessment Authority (1996) *A Guide to the National Curriculum*. London: HMSO.

Stipek, D H (1993) *Motivation to Learn: From Theory to Practice* (2nd ed). Boston: Allyn and Bacon.

Survey Monkey (2012) www.surveymonkey.com (last accessed 8 June 2012).

Twomey Fosnot, C (ed) (1996) *Constructivism Theory, Perspectives and Practice*. New York: Teachers College Press.

Waterhouse, A (1993) The National Curriculum in a Primary school, in M Barber and D Graham (ed) *Sense, Nonsense and the National Curriculum*. London: Falmer Press.

Woolfolk, A (2007) *Educational Psychology*. London: Pearson Publishing.

Woolfolk, A, Hughes, M and Walkup, V (2008) *Psychology in Education*. London: Pearson Publishing.

Chapter 8

The IPC: a return to 1970s-style trendy teaching methods? Certainly not!

Malcolm Davis

The background

In 2007, fear once again arose that primary schools in England were abandoning traditional subjects in favour of 'themed' teaching on topics as varied as chocolate and space travel. This followed a poll of 115 schools by the *Times Educational Supplement* which showed a trend away from subject-based lessons to a theme-based approach to teaching (Ward and Bloom, 2007). A landmark report 15 years earlier had already argued that topic-based classes led to 'fragmentary and superficial teaching' (Alexander *et al*, 1992).

When I was teaching in schools in Bristol and Leeds in the late 1960s and early 1970s Bruner's 'spiral curriculum' was entering the educational conversation. Now in the twilight of my time in schools, as educational leader at the International School of Bremen (ISB), we have in place the International Primary Curriculum (IPC). This is based upon the constructivist approach to learning of which Bruner was one of the original proponents. The IPC acknowledges the thinking of Howard Gardner as one educational philosophy that guides the programme; few know, however, that Gardner was once a young researcher assigned to Bruner or that they worked together on the MACOS (Man: a Course of Study) project (MACOS, 2012). This project focused on the idea that human beings are unique and tried to investigate what makes them unique, seeking to develop ways through which humans could learn to be more human! (Bruner, 1966: 74). In *The Process of Education*, Bruner placed a greater emphasis on learning. His focus was the role of structure in learning and how it might be made central to teaching; the idea that there was a readiness to learn, the nature of intuitive and analytical thinking and, finally, the motives that underpin learning (Bruner, 1960).

This focus on 'humanness' and the qualities that make us human is perhaps even more relevant today as the 21st century gathers momentum – particularly in terms of the importance of structure in the 'process of education': that is, a concern to put learning at the centre of educational activity. In the 1960s and 1970s concern focused on teaching and not on 'looking for learning'. From this perspective Bruner could be considered to have been a trumpeting herald of the International Primary Curriculum. Bruner argued that learners construct their own ideas and understanding based on their existing knowledge (which reminds us of the need now for an IPC knowledge harvest). This might seem self-evident today; too many educational activities at that time, however, saw – and some still see – the student as an empty vessel waiting to be filled up by the actions of the teacher. Contrary to this empty vessel view, the International Primary Curriculum (IPC) argues that at the beginning of teaching a unit of work, a gathering of class knowledge should take place (a knowledge harvest) so that the new learning builds upon the conceptual and knowledge base that the students already have.

The challenge that faces teachers, students and parents involved in the IPC is, I believe, to continue the work begun so long ago and to create an effective development of learning that reflects Bruner's spiral approach and has humans at its heart.

Behavioural sciences

The IPC asserts that it reflects some of the recent findings of the behavioural sciences in that it is 'brain friendly'. It is argued that our knowledge and understanding of how the brain works are increasing at a considerable rate, to the extent that we have perhaps gained more knowledge in this area in the last 15 years than in all previous years. Any educational programme that claims to reflect such a rapidly growing and changing knowledge base must therefore be dynamic in nature. Fortunately for the IPC, it does not involve students in the teenage years; our understanding of the teenage brain is radically changing, so much so that some would argue that educational programmes have to be totally transformed to accommodate our new understandings (Abbott, 2010: 52-53). In terms of the pre-teenage years, brain science (Greenspan, 1997; Strauch, 2003; Abbott, 2006) reveals that cognitive development and conceptual understanding have moved beyond the Piagetian and Bloomian ideas of a hierarchical framework (Anderson and Krathwohl, 2001) reflective of maturation. We now appreciate that even small children can analyse and synthesise as well as evaluate. It is encouraging to see in some of the IPC mileposts acknowledgement of the sophisticated thinking that pre-teenagers can bring to the classroom.

Part of the IPC approach to learning is simply good practice, while other aspects reflect a constructivist approach and a less teacher-centred classroom. This difference alone can challenge the teacher to change, but such a focus on learning rather than teaching does not necessarily let the teacher off the hook. It does, however, require teachers to change what they do (though I wonder whether some can, or even wish to, adapt or adjust to these new perspectives). Learning in schools needs to be intentional – otherwise, why have a school (since, of course, learning does occur in other places and at other times). Thus, teachers must still create an intentional, controlled environment for learning. Teachers, I would also insist, have to change in response to brain research. The idea that we all possess many learning styles and choose one to suit the circumstances or, in some cases, are limited to a few learning styles, has an impact on classroom activity. Reference is made to only three learning styles within the IPC guidelines (auditory, visual, kinaesthetic), yet there might well be many more for which the teacher should cater (see, for instance, www.learning-styles-online.com/overview/).

It could well be concluded that some models of learning are not constructivist in their perspective (Kolb, 1984) though Kolb, like others, argues that all styles should be encountered. As with many models of learning, therefore, it is crucial for the teacher to create an effective learning environment, rather than concentrating on an effective teaching environment. For some this might seem a huge leap away from a traditional classroom set-up. The role of teachers, and the need for them to be learners themselves, will be discussed later.

Student learning

The IPC offers a defined curriculum of study for students through primary/elementary education. Such divisions within schools vary across educational cultures. It is interesting to note that the defined IPC mileposts try to avoid cultural labelling and take the age of students as their guide: the first milepost at age seven, the next at age nine and the third at age 12. At ISB we have placed the IPC across two educational divisions. Milepost 1 begins in our Early Learning Centre (a class of five to six-year-olds) and mileposts finish with the end of Grade 5 (a class of 10 to 11-year-olds). Students below age five are in the early years programme of what I consider to be the IPC, and Grade 6 students (11 to 12-year-olds) now begin with the new International Middle Years Curriculum (IMYC).

Developmentally the IPC spans a huge range. At ISB we face the challenge of introducing ideas such as 'treasure' or 'transport' in units of work to students who certainly cannot read or write (because of their age: three to five-year-olds), and yet they can talk and express themselves and their thinking. Their presentations are short and the evaluations are simple yet effective, and often powerful. They are most comfortable with what they like – if not what they know and fully understand – and even the youngest rise to the challenge of the 'why' question. They can, surprisingly, always justify their position. Trying to get them to articulate their learning is demanding, and might for many be beyond the realms of possibility, but it is rewarding and in keeping with the commitment to stimulate their learning and extend their understanding.

Some of our parents question such rigour in thinking, as they see play as unstructured and certainly not intentionally extending their child's thinking. (It is interesting to note that in our local national schools unstructured play dominates until the age of six.) Some years ago the spiral of revisiting related ideas as students progressed through the school was well developed in some national and international environments. This approach has now been somewhat diminished, I think, as a result of increased teacher autonomy replacing a more centrally or administratively controlled development approach. It is clear that if the milepost objectives are adhered to then skills and conceptual understanding will be developed in a spiral way, being revisited and enhanced as maturity levels increase. This is one of the great strengths of the IPC. The less random approach means that the learning of previous years, conceptually and in terms of skills, becomes the basis for the future. The pressure is on the IPC coordinator not only to map units in order to prevent repetition, but also to collate the content that will become the knowledge harvest base for a future activity. Consequently, skills and conceptual understandings are guided by mileposts while the teacher, within a framework established by the IPC coordinator, can choose units that might reflect the interests of the students. The extent to which each student's individual and collective interest might guide units and the interrelations of units may be questioned, because in some primary programmes collective interest guides all activities – whereas within the IPC it is the task of the teacher to create or inspire interest. There is some truth in the proposition that a good teacher can interest students in anything, but we are not all always 'good teachers'. It takes a confident teacher to allow students free rein to pursue *their* interests when these interests might be tangential to the actual unit.

My observation across many classrooms suggests that certain topics become standard units because at certain ages they are inherently interesting to primary students. Is it mere coincidence for instance that, even though the teacher changes and there is no universally fixed plan, Grade 3 students study a unit involving dinosaurs? Learning activities vary but the content remains much the same. Students at this age are excited by 'monsters' from the distant past and within this context they develop skills and understandings. I have observed learning activities as varied as teachers' interests and skills; from films making use of models to show the discovery of dinosaur skeletons to the construction of a class museum with fossils and reconstructions.

Similarly, Chocolate is a unit of the IPC. Many decades ago the focus in this topic in, for instance, primary schools in England would have been not on the product but more on trade and the interdependence of children in England with colonies and the Empire, from where chocolate originated and how it came to England. There was then no mention of chocolate's origins or the cultures of Central America. Now, through the IPC, students are challenged to see the interconnectivity of ideas through the study of chocolate. History and science are combined, so in-depth knowledge of Aztec culture is encountered along with the way in which chocolate bars are made, flavoured and marketed. I have to admit, though, that I am yet to become accustomed to the garlic-flavoured Choco Bars the director always seems to have to test: our recent chocolate shop in Grade 3 produced 15 different flavours of chocolate bars, each costing 25 cents. This is not only, or even most importantly, a sure way to raise money for charity and stress a sense of community involvement; it is also an almost peerless way to seriously challenge one's sense buds! Some schools find that the unit's knowledge harvest reveals little foundation knowledge but agree that it is a good vehicle through which to develop both knowledge and skills.

In the early years of the 21st century, some expressed fears of a return to 1970s-style teaching, with primary schools abandoning traditional subjects in favour of 'themed' teaching on topics as varied as chocolate and space travel (Ward and Bloom, 2007). This fear rested on an assumption that such unit-based or theme-based approaches would again bring a lowering of standards in literacy and numeracy, after topic-based classes were blamed for collapsing literacy and numeracy standards as teachers shunned the basics. The 1992 landmark report of the so-called 'Three Wise Men' argued that topic-based classes led to 'fragmentary and superficial teaching' (Alexander *et al*, 1992). What is often ignored or forgotten is that literacy and numeracy hours can be combined within the IPC units. Students at ISB, and elsewhere I believe, begin the day with mathematics and English and then go off into themed work or specialist activities (which will be explored later). The strength of this approach is in the structures provided by the IPC in terms of mileposts which allow teachers to focus on creativity without losing sight of attainment levels.

Despite the concern expressed by some in June 2007 at the concept of a unit on space travel as an area of study without substance, the IPC unit Mission to Mars and Beyond remains extremely popular. Considerable amounts of science and technology can be investigated within this unit, which puts learning within a specific and relevant contextual framework. David Hart, former general secretary of the UK National Association of Head Teachers, argued in 2007 that 'theme-based education will disadvantage pupils in the transition to secondary … and it will make the secondary teacher's task much more difficult' (Ward and Bloom, 2007). This challenge is, I think, well met by the newly-developing International Middle Years Curriculum (IMYC, 2011). Through the IMYC, many of the good practices of primary education are carried forward into the secondary school environment. The contrast between IMYC and IPC is significant, however, in terms of types of topics or themes that create contextual frameworks. In the IPC (naturally, for young children) units and guiding themes are concrete in nature – the investigator, the physical world or toys – whereas in the IMYC overarching themes are more abstract, such as adaptability, structure or balance. It is the secondary school that is being given the opportunity to change in response to the new approach to learning within the primary programme. Therefore the secondary cry, "they learn no history or geography in primary, they just do transport and space", is eliminated as the mileposts are subject-skill driven. The skills of history and science are met in a more meaningful context.

Mileposts and teacher learning

Mileposts that delineate learning for each of the three sections (up to age seven, up to age nine and up to age 12) create an attainment structure for the teacher.

A framework of activities is linked, giving the teacher confidence to focus on learning. Discussion with a primary teacher at ISB revealed the great emphasis placed upon establishing through the knowledge harvest what the students already know, what gaps need to be filled and how this will be achieved. This approach allows for significant learner autonomy, but also raises for the teacher the issue of how to extend and build upon already established learning. It is not re-teaching or even reinforcement, but more a scaffolding structure founded upon firm learning which allows the student to climb safely to new levels of learning. The challenge for the teacher in this context is to have the courage and insight to encourage individual students to go as high as they desire and then be challenged to go further. Too often lessons are set up with specific objectives that limit learning; IPC in the hands of the best practitioners can remove the limits from learning.

Specialist teachers

A broader, more problematic issue arises in relation to specialist teachers within the IPC. The programme is best suited to confident 'renaissance man'-type teachers who naturally bring ideas and learning together within the units. Issues can arise, however, when many activities are shared with specialist teachers. In some schools the class teacher teaches everything – perhaps with the exception of physical education (PE). For us, at ISB, students go off to host country instruction (in our case, German), drama, music, information and communications technology (ICT) and, in the final year of IPC (Grade 5, our 10-going-on-11-year-olds), to French and Spanish as well. The real challenge is to draw these specialists in so that they also develop aspects of the unit under study, and the level of teacher learning necessary is considerable. The reality is often that these specialists are simply not fully aware of the unit activity and plough on with their own content and skills regardless of the greater goal to be pursued. At one level, the answer could be more meetings to integrate specialist teachers into what the classroom teacher is doing, or simply not to have specialist teachers involved in the programme to any great extent. The latter approach does not easily work, though, as specialist activity gives the class teacher preparation time. The former is extremely time-consuming, and particularly draws on the time of specialist teachers as they have to meet with each individual class teacher separately.

In reality, the challenge is largely ignored and specialists remain outside the IPC. A separate programme or programmes run alongside what should be perhaps one holistic approach. This means that the IPC becomes a broad-based integrated science and humanities activity, but was this not one of the shortcomings of the 1970s approach? Given the emphasis that seems to be given by the IPC guides to stressing science learning goals more than others, might there not be an argument for letting science drift off as a specialist activity if staffing would allow it? The impact of specialist activity not only creates the need to involve specialists in a more holistic approach; it also asks questions about the qualities needed of the teachers of the self-contained classroom. Yes, primary/elementary teachers are multiskilled – but do they have/should they have the skill of a team leader? From the specialists' perspective, meanwhile, there would be a need for them to be in as many teams as there are classes: quite a commitment.

The IPC does have a built-in driver – assessment – which could keep specialists in concert with the unit of study. The mileposts are subject-specific and, in our school at least, specialist teachers are required to report students' performance by using these milepost descriptors (though as they are not content-specific, specialist teachers *could* still respond without having interacted with a particular unit of study). Some observers might argue that this driver, with control based on assessment, is inappropriate. I would tend to agree, as assessment should provide information about students' performance, not become the *de facto* director of a programme. There would be a real danger of teaching exclusively to the assessment which is, seemingly, not in the learning-focused spirit of the IPC.

In essence, if specialist teachers are a common feature within schools, then much more work has to be done in educating them to buy in fully to the units and the IPC approach. This is where another level of teacher learning is necessary, as pressure is put on both school structures and the time of teachers to meet, collaborate and coordinate activities. Equally, pressure is put on the IPC coordinator to mould the specialists into a way of thinking that reflects the IPC approach to learning.

Parent learning

In late 2011 the IPC curriculum leadership released guiding questions for schools to share with parents. This, I think, is a first step in relation to parents' learning, as a move to focus attention on their role in the learning process. Some parents believe they have no significant part to play in the formalised learning of their child, which is seen as the province of the school. A parent/school partnership might, if the school is lucky, result in significant positive parental involvement in supporting learning (not just the PTA fundraising); however, our recent experience suggests that parental involvement rarely extends beyond the level of reaction. If parents believe their child has a problem they might well be concerned and seek to be heard. From my current school's perspective (and it has been a similar experience in all my schools, even in 'difficult' ones in Leeds in the 1970s), parents are relatively enthusiastic about discussing their child's progress at parent/teacher conferences in the earlier part of the year. A second such conference though, in spring, is usually relatively poorly attended, and it remains an educational axiom that those parents who most need to attend such a meeting are those who least often appear. The objective, from the parents' perspective, is to find out how well their child is doing; if they think the child is doing well, or do not care, they do not get involved. The desire for positive affirmation of their children's ability and performance dominates, rather than a wish to understand the parental role in learning.

Parental gatherings to explain the ongoing curriculum their child is experiencing are generally poorly attended. At one such meeting recently, the staff outnumbered parents. There are, of course, possible solutions that might address the apparent passivity of parents. In terms of increased involvement in parent/teacher conferences there appears to be a growing trend to have child-led conferences in which s/he leads the discussion and shows off the chosen portfolio of work. This puts a degree of obligation on the parent to attend, the focus can be on what has been learned and it is from the child's perspective. In a sister school I discovered a novel approach in which parents were required to contribute to school activities for a set number of hours. This involvement could include attending curriculum meetings and parent conferences, but could also include the usual attendance at a PTA meeting or other school gathering. At the end of the year children whose parents had fulfilled the requirements were given a reward in an assembly. Such an approach might result in significant moral pressure on parents to be involved. I have not yet tried it and would think carefully before doing so, because this approach does not really address the issue of how to involve parents in learning while increasing their own learning and understanding of what their child is experiencing.

The suggested questions and seeming responses set forth in *Helping your child with their learning* seems primarily a motivational and confidence-building exercise (IPC, 2011). For example, use the word 'yet' regularly: in response to "I cannot do fractions" the parent should say "you cannot do fractions yet". The mantra throughout this short piece is 'I might not be brilliant at everything but I can get better'. This is an exceedingly worthwhile approach, but does not necessarily involve parents in learning.

With guidance from the teacher, parents can develop an appreciation and understanding of the goals and desired learning outcomes, so that they can be an effective third element in the triangle of learning. Parents need to comprehend the essence of IPC; the focus on learning (not on teaching) along with, I think, an increasing move to further autonomy in that learning. They have to grasp the changed role of the teacher to one of facilitator of learning rather than of the almighty imparter of knowledge. Parents need to understand the nature of a classroom as a learning environment. Finally, and perhaps most significantly, they need to realise that their child can increasingly understand how s/he learns best and therefore can play a significant role in guiding his/ her own learning, and growing autonomy in learning. One of the ways we have found of doing this (though we make no claim here for great success) is, at least, to have a booklet – *The most frequently asked question about the IPC* – available for parents. Its aim is to encourage parents to be aware of how we see the IPC and how they, as parents, can work within it. I say we make no claim for great success as IPC is often seen as a subject! 'What is this subject?' is the question most often asked by new parents. Are we getting it wrong, I wonder, or are parents looking for the classic school subjects to dominate and guide their thinking about what their child is doing?

Similarly, when information is given back to parents in the structure of the mileposts they might seem relieved, as the mileposts reflect known subjects. However the response is sometimes along the lines of "how has this happened when they did not do history and science; they were doing chocolate?" Whilst seeing their child enjoying a study of chocolate, parents often fail to see how the mainstream subjects are embedded within the unit of work. At worst they search for blocks of time devoted to classic activities rather than contextually-contained skill development and conceptualisation. We see the same forces emerging in the new International Middle Years Curriculum when parents search for formal assessment in relationship to the presentation of the 'Big Idea' and the student presentation of learning at the end of a unit. "If there is no mark, why spend so much time on it?" I have been asked. The mark or assessment is of course the gauge of success, not the capacity to demonstrate, articulate and share learning. What some parents sometimes seek, and students do too, is a reward for the end product rather than a sense of appreciation that the process is both developmental and cumulative.

Recording student progress

This desire for clear marks and rewards is often seen in parent responses to the way we, under the guidance of the IPC, record progress through the mileposts. Three stages exist in the designated learning goals: beginning, developing and mastering. In simplest terms there is an expectation that the child will first encounter a skill or concept at a beginning level and move, over a period of time, to a position of mastery. On a personal level I wonder about this latter terminology as I would hesitate to claim mastery of anything, and it seems peculiarly out of tune with the recent parent IPC guidelines mentioned earlier, which suggest that 'we can all get better'. The issue of parent comprehension arises, however, with respect to beginning new mileposts. Every two years the child returns to a new beginning, which bemuses many as there is an expectation of continued progress and steady improvement. Here, the mark/assessment perspective comes into play; "If they were getting Cs," parents ask, "then Bs and finally As, how come they now go back to C? What has gone wrong?" Often parents have difficulty in grasping that changed expectations and changed goals will result in changed performance. Learning seemingly returns to a start point. Parents tend to view learning, or what they see as their children's performance, as being on a level field where they simply continue to progress towards the far end. Many do not appreciate that the metaphor of the staircase works better than the metaphor of the playing field, and that every so often there is a need to go up a step. Such a manoeuvre might be very difficult and will perhaps occur for different children at different times. How often have we heard it said "They were doing so well and now they cannot ...". Much as their child's learning might be a continuum in the form of a staircase, so too is the parents' understanding of the programme as their children move through it. It is not surprising that, as we as professionals struggle with understanding the complexity of a child's learning, the parent finds it more difficult – and the over-anxious parent even more so.

The next steps

The International Middle Years Curriculum faces many of the same issues that have been raised about learning in relation to the IPC. We at ISB have yet to see fully (in our first year operating the IMYC) how much teacher learning has to take place. The abstract themes, such as Structure or Adaptability, that lace through conventional class subjects do challenge the teacher and the same questions arise: 'How can I teach Structure when I have this block of grammar to get through and they cannot even speak French yet anyway?' Clearly there is a call for more teacher education and awareness-raising. The parent, even more so with graduation to the secondary school, seeks to hold onto the pastoral care aspects of the classroom teacher in the primary school which, of course, can be diminished in the secondary school context. In contrast parents eagerly seek to see everything marked and evaluated in a formal way just as they experienced in their time at school. Hart's views about theme work noted earlier, and Woodhead's criticism that 'if you want somebody to make progress in a particular subject, you teach them that subject' (in Ward and Bloom, 2007) prevail among parents, in my experience. I wonder how often we have had to explain why we think the end presentation of learning is important and is not just another waste of time away from subject-based learning, and why it will not be formally assessed.

What rests at the heart of the IPC, and now the IMYC, is a belief that everything should pass the litmus test of 'relevance' to the overall learning of the child. Teachers and parents have to buy into this. With all the issues associated with children's learning, both teachers and parents ought to realise that there need be no fear of the watering down of learning with a return to themed learning.

Much more work remains to be done, but increased knowledge of how the brain works, and its consequences for how a child's learning in school is structured, protects our children's time in school from the superficial trendiness of the 1970s approach which perhaps seemed intuitively acceptable but lacked the substance to support its position. Boxed, compartmentalised learning – still the chief characteristic of secondary education – was to return for a time. There is now a realisation, however, that the 21st century child needs a more holistic approach to how knowledge works and how it can be used to investigate and to solve problems. Clearly much work needs to be done to encourage all parties at all levels of education to grasp how we learn best. An ISB student in June 2011, having experienced our trial run of the IMYC, confirmed that a more holistic approach with deliberately planned linking themes does seem to improve understanding, in explaining that "by looking at 'balance' and then having to do my presentation on 'balance' to the rest of the class, I began to understand how all my subjects worked together". Learning in action, indeed, at the highest level.

References

Abbott, J (2006) *Adolescence: A critical evolutionary adaptation*. Bath: The 21st Century Learning Initiative.

Abbott, J (2010) *Over Schooled but Under Educated*. London: Continuum International Publishing Group.

Alexander, R, Rose, J and Woodhead, C (1992) *Curriculum Organisation and Classroom Practice in Primary Schools*. London: DES (Available online via http://www.educationengland.org.uk/documents/threewisemen/).

Anderson, L W and Krathwohl, D M (2001) *A Taxonomy for Learning, Teaching, and Assessing: A Revision of Bloom's Taxonomy of Educational Objectives*. London: Longman.

Bruner, J S (1960) *The Process of Education*. Cambridge, MA: Harvard University Press.

Bruner, J S (1966) *Toward a Theory of Instruction*. Cambridge, MA: Belkapp Press.

Greenspan, S I (1997) *The Growth of the Mind, and the Endangered Origins of Intelligence*. New York: Perseus Books.

IPC (2011) *Helping your child with their learning*. London: International Primary Curriculum.

IMYC (2011) *IMYC Teacher File*. London: International Middle Years Curriculum.

Kolb, D A (1984) *Experiential Learning: Experience as the source of learning and development*. London: Prentice Hall.

MACOS (2012) Accessed online at www.anthro.umontreal.ca/personnel/beaudetf/MACOS/MACOS.html (last accessed 29 May 2012).

Strauch, B (2003) *The Primal Teen: What the new discoveries about the teenage brain tell us about our kids*. New York: Doubleday.

Ward, H and Bloom, A (2007) Creativity back in favour. *Times Educational Supplement*, 8 June 2007.

Chapter 9

Recruiting teachers for IPC schools

Andrew Wigford

Introduction

If we agree with O'Neill (1994) that effective human resource management in education impacts on learning in the classroom and that this is 'dependent on the recruitment, retention and development of professional teachers', then staff selection must be viewed as a crucial part of a school leader's responsibility. This view is reinforced by Adams (1987: 143) who states that 'if the quality of staff is a vital factor for the success of the school, then the right appointment of staff is a vital management exercise'. A good appointment will strengthen the school staff and the teams within it; a bad appointment can have the reverse effect. Many authors, including Wallace and Hall (1997), talk about the value of a cohesive staff, who work towards common goals and buy into its curriculum. It is important that new staff are recruited who fit well into existing teams, have something new to offer them and are prepared to engage in the curriculum. When recruiting, schools should have carefully assessed their needs based on the curriculum. Skelton (1999, in Garton 2000) states that the process of recruitment starts when the school clearly defines staffing needs and allies this to the school's philosophy, goals and curriculum.

More important than facilities, resources, board members and even heads, a school is ultimately judged by the quality of its teaching and learning. The recruitment of the right teachers is therefore crucial. Many heads of school agree with O'Neill, Garton, Skelton (*op. cit.*) and others in seeing recruitment as their most important contribution to the school. After all, many of the teachers recruited will remain in the school long after the head departs, and can have a long-term impact.

Curriculum and recruitment

To what extent should the curriculum a school uses impact on recruitment processes and decision-making regarding so-called 'new hires'? As Skelton (*op. cit.*) points out, recruitment should ideally be guided by the school's philosophy. If a programme such as the International Primary Curriculum (IPC) is to be effectively implemented in a school, it needs teachers who are committed to the programme. Teachers should have the experience and ability to engage children in learning-focused activities, to facilitate specific learning opportunities and to assess accurately whether learning has taken place. The IPC relies to a certain extent on teachers working together closely, particularly in the planning stages. Teachers within the same year group are encouraged to follow the same IPC unit; they may carry out an entry point activity together and share resources. The ability, therefore, to work effectively as part of a team is important.

The IPC encourages children to be actively involved in their learning, with the teacher playing the role of facilitator. Many would argue that only teachers who are experienced and confident are able to give children the time and space to develop their thinking, and to explore fully and formulate their own ideas. Others may argue that only those teachers who have high levels of enthusiasm and energy can work effectively with the IPC. Teachers need to be highly motivated and to have an acute awareness that learning takes place when children are fully engaged and having fun. Some school heads may argue that these are advanced teaching skills, and that finding teachers who are able to implement the programme successfully is a tricky business. Others may say that, as long as the teachers possess certain qualities and the willingness to immerse themselves fully in the IPC, then the rest depends on the school's own induction and training.

A small-scale study

So how do IPC school recruiters find the appropriate teachers for their schools? What do they look for specifically? This chapter describes a piece of research that involved nine experienced IPC school recruiters (mostly, but not all, heads) from different schools based in Europe, The Middle East, Central America and the Far East. Each was asked to complete a short questionnaire based on the following four questions:

1. What kind of training, teaching experience and qualifications would you look for when recruiting IPC teachers?

2. What, in your experience, are the top five characteristics of an effective IPC teacher that you would look for when recruiting?

3. Is prior experience with the IPC an important prerequisite when shortlisting candidates?

4. What process of induction would you recommend for teachers new to your IPC school?

The outcomes of the small-scale study are discussed as follows, with verbatim responses unattributed to protect their anonymity.

Teaching experience and qualifications

Most recruiters first encounter an applicant via a *curriculum vitae* or *resumé*. The study showed that in most cases it appears that the first thing recruiters look for is teaching experience. Two to three years' experience was a minimum expectation of those questioned, and some schools insisted on five or six years since graduating. Having grounding in at least one curriculum programme (the IPC or any other) was considered a useful prerequisite. These years of experience would give teachers the confidence to try new approaches in the classroom and not to treat the curriculum like a manual or a 'straitjacket'. As one respondent pointed out:

"Teachers who find the transition (to the IPC) the easiest are those that have a few years teaching under their belts and have faith in their teaching abilities, and do not hold onto the rigidity of some national systems."

Of course most recruiters look for previous teaching experience with the IPC, but it was acknowledged that these teachers were often few and far between. In fact, one head admitted to never having actually recruited a teacher with previous IPC experience. Interestingly, the majority of those surveyed indicated previous experience with more than one curriculum as highly desirable. For example, teachers who have experienced teaching the national curriculum of England and Wales plus the International Baccalaureate Primary Years Programme (IBPYP) in different schools were targeted by recruiters. Those teachers who had already experienced different programmes were considered better prepared to take on another, as indicated by the following response:

"I generally preferred teachers with [at least] four years' experience and only fully qualified primary teachers. I was also especially interested in candidates who had UK and IBPYP experience because of the similarities between the two programmes, and because it meant they had already experienced taking on a new curriculum."

Specialist qualifications and training in early childhood or primary were considered vital by some schools as well as (in certain countries) a work visa. In some cases the location of a teacher's training was considered a key factor. Teachers trained in the UK, Australia or New Zealand were preferred because, as one recruiter pointed out, the pedagogy of the programmes of these countries was perceived to be closely aligned with the IPC philosophy:

"We shortlist based upon whether we believe the candidate is capable of dealing with multiple curricula. Successful PYP teachers, and teachers from countries with a strong grounding in this kind of pedagogy like New Zealand and Australia, have an advantage."

All those surveyed indicated that good training was important, but not necessarily the most important factor. Once teachers were trained and had appropriate experience, a number of common characteristics were considered important by the recruiters.

Characteristics of good IPC teacher candidates

The survey exposed remarkably common characteristics most sought after in teacher candidates. Top of the list was a focus on learning. The same phrase was used by every single one of the recruiters surveyed. The heads involved in the study all said that they were looking for teachers who were 'passionate about learning' – perhaps hardly surprising given the focus on the learning experience that is central to the very core of the IPC. It is an important part of the IPC philosophy and separates it from other curriculum programmes that, arguably, focus on teaching techniques rather than on children's learning. Teachers who are passionate about promoting learning and who are good learners themselves fit very well into the IPC philosophy and, therefore, into the schools that use the programme. Recruiters stated that they wanted to hear teachers talking about learning at interview; about how they identify and assess learning.

Other commonly identified characteristics in the survey were more typical of those used by recruiters at many other schools around the world, though they are nonetheless interesting when considered in IPC terms. Candidates perceived as confident and outgoing, for instance, were preferred by most recruiters, who argued that IPC teachers need to be confident in their own abilities: they need to be able to accept new ideas about learning and assessment and to be capable of working well in a team. They need to have a 'sense of fun' because the programme offers many opportunities for role play, dressing up and acting. They need to be enthusiastic because the IPC is based on the premise that children can learn best when they are having fun. Candidates who demonstrated confidence and enthusiasm to immerse themselves fully in the programme and to be part of the learning experience themselves were considered highly desirable.

Most of those surveyed described flexibility and open-mindedness as key characteristics in candidates. Many argued that these attributes are important because the programme is still relatively new and unfamiliar to many recruits. A desire to try new ideas and openness to the underlying philosophy of the programme are vital if the teacher is to embrace the programme fully. Some more traditional teaching techniques, such as those that focus on the teacher imparting knowledge, can detract from the important child-centred acquisition of skills and the development of understanding. The IPC teacher, it is argued, should be principally interested in actively involving children in their own learning and promoting learning opportunities. To be effective, IPC teachers should see their role as facilitators for learning. They also need to be skilled in recognising when learning is taking place and when it is not. Such skills are not easy to acquire. They take practice. Some recruiters referred to this point as justification for sometimes selecting more mature teachers. They argued that the IPC requires in teachers higher order skills that are found only in professionals who have been teaching for some time. Others, however, pointed out that a learning-focused curriculum, linked to assessment based on an understanding of how the brain works, is a relatively new concept for many. More experienced teachers may be held back by entrenched ideas and practices that may lead them to resist the programme, whereas new teachers may be more open-minded.

Most of those surveyed also highlighted a need for candidates to be internationally-minded and able to demonstrate some understanding of what this means. The IPC programme places a large emphasis on developing international-mindedness. In fact it was one of the first curriculum programmes in the world to identify specific learning outcomes for international-mindedness, linking these to activities that present learning opportunities. It is no wonder then that some understanding of what this means to candidates is believed to be important and that recruiters refer to it at interview. How this attribute was to be measured, however, was less clear.

Prior experience with the IPC programme

Most IPC schools include prior experience with the programme as a desirable prerequisite when advertising vacancies. Teachers who have this experience will have a distinct advantage when it comes to shortlisting from a large pool of candidates. However, as noted earlier, such teachers can be hard to find. Those surveyed quoted as equally important the characteristics mentioned above. Candidates who demonstrate a clear empathy with the principles of the programme and its underlying philosophy – either through their training or from experience with other curricula – were considered highly desirable, as were those who demonstrate openness to new ideas and obvious enthusiasm to take the IPC on board.

It may be true to say that teachers trained in thematic approaches to learning in countries such as the UK and Australia in the 1980s are well prepared to engage in the IPC approach. It could also be true, however, that these teachers are familiar with a style of teaching and learning that has now changed beyond recognition. Teachers who are more recently qualified and trained in an arguably more rigorous approach, based on learning goals and measured outcomes, may find the IPC more recognisable. Most school recruiters in the survey tried to look for a balance in terms of experience and ability. They consider the team as a whole and ensure that they have the right mix of maturity and expertise, as noted by one respondent:

> "When putting together a staff team it is more important to have a balance of skills and experience to make the team effective. Experience with the IPC is not always a prerequisite when shortlisting."

Some heads indicated that, occasionally, prior experience with the IPC could actually be a disadvantage if that experience had been in schools where the programme was used ineffectively:

> "In the past we have had some teachers with IPC experience but they did not necessarily believe in the philosophy so it just becomes mediocre topic teaching. By comparison, we recently employed an Australian teacher who

had no prior experience but all the right characteristics, and after a brief induction was able to quickly capture the essence of the programme."

Of course this is probably true for any curriculum. Teachers may be able to cite previous experience with a programme but may not have fully embraced or understood its philosophy. Likewise they may not have had the chance to experience good quality training during their induction.

The process of induction

Good induction implemented effectively can have a remarkable effect on the speed with which a new employee settles in, and starts well before the teacher arrives at the school. Garton (2000) refers to the period just after a job offer has been accepted as the 'follow-up and settling-in or orientation phase'. This is based on the belief that staff induction begins during the interview and then carries on when the new teacher arrives at the school and well into the first year of their contract. Between signing the contract and taking up their post, teachers who are new to the programme should be encouraged to start their IPC learning; to attend IPC summer courses (if possible) and to keep in close email contact with year group colleagues who can share with them route maps and units to study. Many of those surveyed outlined the importance of providing new staff with IPC handbooks, units and policy manuals before their arrival in the new school. Once teachers were successfully recruited, most of the heads surveyed highlighted the importance of good quality induction – whether or not the teacher had prior IPC experience. Some relied on external training courses such as the summer camps and regional courses run by the IPC organisation. Others championed training run by their own experienced practitioners.

Mentoring with new staff was widely used by the schools surveyed. New teachers were encouraged to observe lessons in the classrooms of more experienced colleagues, and time for weekly meetings and reflection was allocated, as indicated by one recruiter:

"We would always have an induction period planned into the timetable to ensure that we are definitely on the same page regarding the school's philosophy / learning policy, and allow them to become familiar with the school's chosen route map and planning and assessment approaches."

This kind of induction is vital for teachers new to the school. It presents an opportunity for experienced IPC teachers to find out how the programme is implemented at this school and for novices to become acclimatised to the teaching context. Spreading the induction programme over a few weeks or months is also very sensible. Often teachers new to international schools have to deal with a number of relocation issues including accommodation and employment visas, making it difficult for them to concentrate on curriculum issues. Too many schools try to force as much induction as possible into a few days before the start of term at a time when the new member of staff has so much on his/her mind. One respondent pointed out that:

> "We arrange an in-house IPC induction programme run by our own IPC Coordinators. The first sessions cover the basics of getting started with the IPC, then a second session a few weeks later looks at international-mindedness and then a third goes into finer details."

The importance of good staff induction cannot be overestimated. Once a teacher has been successfully recruited, the next task is to make sure he/she can effectively deliver the curriculum aligned to the school's philosophy.

Conclusion

The IPC is a relatively new programme that has grown rapidly in popularity over the last ten years. Recruiting teachers for schools that have adopted the programme is a challenge, which is not always straightforward for those heads who are concerned to recruit teachers who can easily fit in with its philosophy. Finding teachers with prior IPC experience can be difficult, and this small-scale survey shows that many recruiters rely on hiring teachers who demonstrate certain key characteristics and then back this up with a well-structured induction programme.

The ways in which schools identify these key characteristics are less clear. Many will rely on evaluation of training, prior experience and references written by other heads. If an agency is used, it may also be possible to draw on the knowledge a recruitment consultant has of the candidate. A lot will then depend on the responses the candidate gives to questions at interview. Most interviews are about an hour in length, although they can be much less at international school recruitment fairs (Wigford, 2002). If well structured, interviews can be revealing, but in the short space of time available they are unlikely to provide a wholly accurate picture of a candidate.

As soon as the teacher accepts a job offer and signs a contract, the 'orientation period' referred to by Garton (*op. cit.*) becomes all-important, especially for schools that are using a curriculum unfamiliar to new recruits. This period includes a well thought-out induction programme that lasts throughout the first year of a teacher's employment. It will involve mentoring, in-house training and external training. Implementing such a programme is time-consuming and can be quite expensive, but should be given high priority. If combined with a rigorous recruitment process, it should produce members of staff who make a significant and long-term contribution to the school in general and to its implementation of the IPC in particular.

Acknowledgements

The author would like to thank the following schools for taking part in this study and for the advice and support they provided: St John's International

School Bangkok; the International Department of the HSV Primary School (part of the Stichting Haagsche Schoolvereeniging); The British School of Costa Rica; Antwerp British School; Compass International School Doha; Compass International School, Al Khor; Amsterdam International Community School; PDO School, Muscat; and the International Academy – Amman.

References

Adams, N (1987) *Secondary School Management Today*. London: Hutchinson Education.

Garton, B (2000) *Recruitment of teachers for international education*, in M Hayden and J Thompson (eds) *International Schools and International Education: improving teaching, management and quality*. London: Kogan Page.

O'Neill, J (1994) Managing Human Resources, in T Bush and J West-Burnham (eds) *The Principles of Educational Management*. London: Paul Chapman Publishing.

Wallace, M and Hall, V (1997) The Dynamics of Teams, in M Crawford, L Kydd and C Riches (eds) *Leadership and Teams in Educational Management*. Buckingham: Open University Press.

Wigford, A (2002) *Employment Interviews at Two International Schools Job Fairs: perceptions of recruiters and candidates*. University of Bath: unpublished MA in Education dissertation.

Chapter 10

Teaching assistants: providing support for the IPC

Estelle Tarry

Introduction

It is widely recognised that teaching assistants increasingly play a role in supporting children's learning in the classroom (Walton and Goddard, 2009; Rose and Forlin, 2010; Tarry, 2011). In the UK, the school workforce reform initiative introduced in 2003 has led to a marked increase in the number of teaching assistants in schools (Audit Commission, 2011). In the context of international schools, Hayden and Thompson (2011) point out that increases in the number of such schools is accompanied by expatriate teachers becoming more difficult to recruit. There is thus a possibility that international schools will become increasingly reliant on locally hired teachers and possibly teaching assistants, both local and expatriate. Rose and Forlin (2010) highlighted through their research that 'additional staffing may be necessary to enable teachers to be more effective in supporting a diverse range of student needs in classrooms' (p311). In the context of the International Primary Curriculum (IPC), offered as it is in both national and international schools, it is important to consider the knowledge, understanding and skills required by teaching assistants (TAs) if they are to support children, support IPC best practice and make it more accessible to learners. TAs need to be aware of 'best practice' in providing a purposeful learning environment, where 'best practice', for this chapter, will be viewed in terms of supporting learning and teaching with a positive impact on students' experiences.

This chapter will also highlight the challenges faced by TAs in supporting learners through the IPC, including how to create a purposeful learning environment, and how to meet the needs of all children including those with special educational needs, those who have English as an additional language, and those who are categorised as gifted and talented. The deployment of TAs to support the IPC will also be addressed, giving suggestions for overcoming challenges faced. For the purpose of this chapter the term teaching assistant (TA) will encompass other related terms including learning support assistant, learning support mentor and classroom assistant.

IPC learning environment and the teaching assistant

The role of the TA has evolved from supporting the teacher with photocopying resources, washing paintbrushes and monitoring playtimes to responsibilities including pastoral care and specifically supporting children in their learning. The role now includes assisting with the specific taught curriculum as well as the more hidden aspects of the curriculum, including values and expectations of the school community. In the case of the IPC this includes learning, personal and international goals, and core values. The role of the TA has expanded to embody a wide range of roles, varying across the age range of children, from school to school and from country to country.

Lawrence (2009) highlights the importance of TAs supporting the teacher in providing a purposeful learning environment. He suggests that if a purposeful learning environment is provided then children will be encouraged to reach their full potential. In the international school context, Haldimann and Hollington point out that 'our role as international educators is to value differences and create school environments where different students' needs are accommodated' (2004: 10). The TA can offer support for that role.

The IPC recommends a sequence of thematic units which ensures that all subjects and learning goals are covered. By using the IPC route planner, teachers may opt to select topics that are particularly relevant to the experience and needs of their children, and interweave the IPC learning goals relating to Mileposts 1, 2 and 3, and knowledge, skills and understanding, to form a curriculum relevant to the context of the particular school. Schools do not need to be constrained by the suggested routes. By ensuring that teaching assistants are not on the periphery of decision-making, but are a central part of the team involved in the unit choice process and in the self-evaluation and any external review, the IPC core values and goals are more likely to be embedded in the school and in the learning. TAs may well be already established in the local community and possibly be expert in local information and local resources. This local knowledge can be used to ensure that the units are appropriate and that children receive their full entitlement to the whole curriculum. The IPC units can be adapted for the individual country in which the school is located, through for instance Weather and Climate (Milepost 3, 9-12 years). Careful consideration needs to be given to content: whether snow and frost should be included, for instance, if the children have never experienced such conditions – though by the same argument perhaps Dinosaurs (Before People) should not be covered, and yet children invariably find this topic interesting and inspiring!

The IPC has been developed to 'engage and inspire' the learner. When units span between four and eight weeks, however, for some children (and possibly teachers) boredom and motivation may become an issue. The TA can encourage inclusion through curriculum development, motivation and support.

IPC and the teaching assistant supporting children's learning

The main responsibility of a TA is to 'support the child in all areas of the curriculum' (Birkett, 2008). TAs need to support a diverse range of children experiencing the IPC including, as noted above, those with special educational needs, those who have English as an additional language, and the gifted and talented. Differentiation can be provided through support, activity and resources, time spent on activity, learning outcomes and learning styles. TAs can assist differentiation through providing specific help either on a one-to-one basis or through group work, through questioning and clear instructions, through modelling, developing higher/lower order thinking activities and making/adapting resources according to children's abilities and learning styles. TAs can correct misconceptions and prevent the spread of misconceptions through the class, especially perhaps during the transition from one unit to another.

Blatchford *et al* (2012), following their research on the impact of TAs, suggest that TAs do not always understand the concepts they are supposed to be helping children to acquire and do not always provide the best support for children if, for instance, they simply give children the answers. A close working relationship with teachers therefore needs to be established. Once TAs are trained and skilled, however, they are able to support children who may have difficulties with certain IPC key concepts within a theme, but are still expected to make connections. Connections within a theme may also be missed if, for instance, children miss a day or are withdrawn for extra support. TAs can, again, provide support with this central aspect of the IPC.

IPC and the teaching assistant promoting individual learning

Lawrence (2009) suggests that learning is most effective when learners take responsibility for their own learning. Although Blatchford *et al* (2012) found that TAs did not always support the development of children's independence and that initiations by children resulted in better understanding, the IPC provides the TA with opportunities to adopt a supportive role enabling children to be more engaged and inspired in their learning and more likely to reach their full potential. The IPC encourages children to follow their interests and to research for information. Not all children already have the relevant research skills, however, and these need to be taught. Oliver (2004) raises the issue of promoting children's research skills and encouraging them to write 'in your own words', questioning the relevance of re-composing information. In the IPC context, the TA can employ strategies to support IPC delivery by introducing ICT in learning activities and independence in its use.

TAs need to be aware of the importance of intercultural communication, the challenges presented by working with different languages, and cultural issues arising in different contexts. In the context of international schools, Codrington makes a salient point in reminding us that 'given the extreme diversity of students in most international schools, with their wide range of cultural, linguistic and religious perspectives as well as varying traditions towards the process of learning, 'best practice' requires that recognition be given to individual differences among students' (2004: 183).

The IPC offers opportunities for teachers and TAs to provide feedback to children through the IPC formal recording rubrics that enable teachers and TAs to describe children's performance using the beginning, developing and mastering learning goals across the eight subjects and international-mindedness. Through discussion, questioning and observation, the TA can provide support by adjusting activities according to the children's understanding, progress and recorded achievements.

Blatchford *et al* (2012) found that TAs, on the whole, only used prompts and different types of questioning. The IPC, however, enables the TA to cater for different learning styles by using different IPC activities, underpinned by Gardner's theories of multiple intelligences (2006). Providing TAs with opportunities to link prior knowledge through discussion, conversation, raising open-ended questions, explanation of concepts and misconceptions, and reinforcing the IPC learning goals is consistent with Blatchford *et al*'s findings that these strategies contribute to cognitive engagement. With appropriate support and training TAs can adopt strategies promoting IPC's philosophy of individual learning.

IPC and the teaching assistant supporting children with special educational needs

The IPC has three levels of entry (beginning, developing and mastering) that allow children to start at a level suitable to their needs. The TA may need, however – in conjunction with the teacher – to adapt IPC activities in order to enable children with special educational needs to access the IPC, if they need to develop more basic functional skills. TAs working in small groups, encouraging children to interact and work cooperatively with others, can engage all children in IPC activities. Consider a lesson, for instance, which includes the IPC Mind Map activity initiated at the beginning of the unit. The activity can be adapted by the TA in working with the group and encouraging each individual to come up with one known fact and write it simply on a Post-it note, then combining all the facts so generated on to one large mind map. One challenging issue here is the adaptation of materials to an accessible level for a particular child with special needs, as this requires specific knowledge and a deep understanding of the individual. As Blatchford *et al* (2012) highlight, TAs may have a good personal understanding of the child; this can make the role of the TA vital in the support and delivery of the IPC.

Burgess and Shelton Mayes point out that 'many teaching assistants are deployed to work specifically with children with social, emotional and behavioural problems and therefore have a key role in ensuring inclusion in primary mainstream classrooms' (2009: 4). In the case of a child with autism, for instance, and an interest in trains, in order to maintain the child's interest during the unit The Active Planet (Earthquakes and Volcanoes), the TA may plan to investigate train stations/tracks near a specific volcano.

Emotional issues also need to be considered and addressed by the TA, since (as has actually happened in my own experience) when the point is made that erupting volcanoes, earthquakes and tsunamis may cause destruction and possibly death, an autistic child may become distressed and anxious. In the case in question this led to the TA being particularly sensitive when the unit Before People (Dinosaurs) was studied, as the autistic child became anxious in response to the news that dinosaurs are now extinct.

To accommodate deaf children, other resources can be located to support IPC. In the case of the same unit, websites are available where details of volcanoes can be inserted and a visual representation of an eruption presented. Arguably, resources such as these are useful for all children. Locating and sometimes making resources takes time of course, which means that the TA's face-to-face time supporting children could be limited. Such support does, however, release the teacher to concentrate on the learning and teaching of the whole class, which Blatchford *et al* (2012) strongly advocate is important in all children accessing the curriculum.

IPC and the teaching assistant supporting children with English as an additional language

In a multicultural classroom context the TA, due to the children's differing cultural and ethnic backgrounds, needs to provide sensitive support that takes into consideration the different non-verbal language, body language and paralanguage exhibited within the class. One challenge of the IPC is to ensure that a variety of vocabulary is used and that language is not just aimed at one theme. TAs, both within groups and on a one-to-one basis, need to develop and explore language. The IPC extends beyond the language structure of sounds and grammar, so the TA needs to bring the IPC thematic knowledge together and to make sense of a whole developing narrative. By using the IPC mind maps, children's previous knowledge and experience can be developed, and with the aid of IPC resources such as photographs, explanation, modelling and strategies such as open-ended questioning, can be used to support, develop and assess learning. In the context of the unit The Things People Do, for instance, and an activity on Jobs with Year 1 children, the TA can work with a small group supporting reading and role-playing people at work which, with guidance, questioning and discussion, can assist with EAL children's oral development.

In the multicultural English-medium classroom, with children whose first language may not be English and who have no support in English at home or in their environment, a vital role for the TA can be in developing alternative materials for non-native speakers of English, transferring skills from the child's mother tongue to learning English and, where appropriate, using local language to support the child in early years. Reflecting on IPC word banks, both English and the child's mother tongue can be used and TAs can ensure that children with EAL are exposed to a variety of language, not just focusing on the IPC theme.

TAs may be able to support word banks for the IPC themes in more than one language. It could be argued that there is benefit to employing TAs specifically to support a minority language or, in an international school, employing a TA whose mother tongue is the local language. By supporting the first language of a non-native English speaker and enabling the child to hear his or her own language, the development of the child's self-esteem can be supported too. The TA can also, where appropriate, ensure that the materials and resources, including the English texts used to support the IPC, do not require prior knowledge of, for instance, Anglo Saxon/Christian culture. Again, communication and a good relationship between teacher and TA is valuable as 'the talking through of cross-curricular issues in a professional development forum will ease tensions and avoid the tendency towards prescriptive and presumptive stands on either the language or subject content of a course' (Burke, 2009: 30).

IPC and the teaching assistant enriching the curriculum

Children identified as gifted and talented also need to be supported if they are to reach their full potential. The IPC endeavours to provide for this group of children by allowing TAs the opportunity to enrich the curriculum through facilitating extension activities. If TAs are to do this effectively they need to develop productive working relationships with the children, have high expectations and develop extending activities that promote higher order thinking skills such as problem solving. Reflecting on a lesson on volcanoes, for instance, the TA can work with the children to develop higher order questions that the children can investigate, while ensuring that information discovered by the children is accurate. This is of course a general issue with searching on the internet, and children need to be able to recognise accurate information by being aware of the status of different websites.

Through the IPC, opportunities are provided for promoting and encouraging open-mindedness, respect for other cultures, beliefs, values and opinions, and celebration of diversity and commonality. The IPC enables TAs to recognise and identify the learning, personal and international goals, and to be able to model the core values to children. The IPC can take advantage of TAs' specialist curricular, learning and teaching areas. Utilising the TA's specialist skills, such as playing an instrument, training and experience, can enrich the content support and delivery of the IPC for those identified as gifted and talented, as well as for children more generally.

IPC and the teaching assistant supporting the school ethos

As Haldimann and Hollington (2004) point out, a curriculum is more than just a collection of subjects: it is about creating a whole school ethos. TAs are part of the mutually supportive learning community that is a school and as such should be part of the school's shared and 'stated' vision (Codrington, 2004). Fail (2011) suggests that to be international we need to share international goals, while Bunnell (2010) describes the 'global dimension' embedded in UK and international policy. In the same way, the IPC international goals should be embedded and not perceived as an add-on.

The IPC enables the TA to support international-mindedness and international perspectives. As Fail points out: 'It is important to acknowledge that people do share different values, world views, behaviours and traditions according to their background' (2011: 102-103). Depending on the context, TAs may be in an ideal position to promote school/community links and to ensure that cultural diversity is embedded in the school ethos. This may involve organising and supporting social events with the local community that link into IPC themes such as Dressing up (Clothes) for Year 2 children and local/national celebrations that include wearing different national costumes. Some might argue that putting national costume in the class dressing-up box devalues those cultures in some way, and the role of the TA in such a context can be important in ensuring international-mindedness and respect is maintained. TAs can also support school trips which link into the units; for example the topic on Dinosaurs could entail, depending on the school context, a visit to the Natural History Museum, while the Flowers and Insects unit could include a visit to a butterfly farm.

Deploying teaching assistants to support IPC 'best practice'

TAs can support and enrich the IPC, if their professional skills are recognised and are deployed effectively. To ensure that the IPC is implemented effectively and the IPC school ethos embedded throughout, school leaders need to address the training and deployment of TAs. Burgess and Shelton Mayes (2009: 4) highlight challenges in 'raising the professional status of teaching assistants' and argue that 'effective training programmes are essential to promote the role'. More recently, Rose and Forlin (2010) suggested that not only is the role of school leaders important in ensuring the appropriate deployment of TAs, as well as TAs themselves being aware of their role and expectations; there is also the need for teachers to be aware of the potential effectiveness of deploying TAs. Arguably, therefore, a holistic approach is required if TAs are to play an effective role in ensuring that implementation of the IPC is successful.

No matter where a school is located, deployment of TAs in supporting the IPC can be a consideration. Hayden and Thompson (2011) suggest that as the nature of international schools becomes increasingly diverse and many national schools have increasingly multicultural populations, the differences between national and international schools are gradually being eroded. 'If we accept children from all parts of the globe, we are already accepting children with different needs,' write Haldimann and Hollington (2004: 1). TAs can provide a supportive role for children from any background in any context in which the IPC is offered.

Conclusion

Many generic issues arise when TAs are involved in supporting any curriculum, including planning and interpreting others' plans, time management, access to records, communication, limited resources and motivation. The IPC includes strategies that, if managed and implemented appropriately, can effectively deal with such issues. Whole-school timetabling needs to be considered to ensure that school facilities such as the ICT suite and outside learning space are accessible by all as needed. Blatchford *et al*'s (2012) research into the impact of teaching assistants suggests that the TA's role is to support the curriculum (in this case, the IPC) by adopting a 'complementary' role to that of the teacher. The TA, by using IPC activities along with IPC-created extension activities to cater for children whose capabilities lie all along the academic spectrum, can ensure that children do not need to be withdrawn from the mainstream curriculum. The teacher can lead the whole class, thus maintaining teacher/child contact and promoting inclusion and acceptance of all pupils. 'TAs and teachers need to strike a delicate balance in order to promote academic engagement, but not at the cost of social interactions with peers and the teachers,' writes Whitehorn (2010: 46). The IPC empowers teaching assistants by making available opportunities to provide support and encouragement for children and by promoting a positive learning environment for all.

References

Audit Commission (2011) *The wider workforce; Better value for money*. London: Audit Commission.

Birkett, V (2008) *Survive and succeed as a teaching assistant*. Cambridge: LDA Publishers.

Blatchford, P, Russell, A and Webster, R (2012) *Reassessing the impact of teaching assistants; How research challenges practice and policy*. Abingdon: Routledge.

Bunnell, T (2010) The momentum behind the International Primary Curriculum in schools in England. *Journal of Curriculum Studies*, 42 (4) 471-486.

Burgess, H and Shelton Mayes, A (2009) An exploration of higher level teaching assistants' perceptions of their training and development in the context of school workforce reform. *Support for Learning*, 24 (1) 19–25.

Burke, L (2009) Engaging with the foundations of literacy – supporting ESL and EAL students across the international school curriculum. *International Schools Journal*, 24 (1) 26-37.

Codrington, S (2004) Applying the concept of 'best practice' to international schools. *Journal of Research in International Education*, 3 (2) 173–188.

Fail, H (2011) Teaching and learning in international schools, in R Bates (eds), *Schooling internationally; Globalisation, internationalisation and the future for international schools*. Abingdon: Routledge [112-115].

Gardner, H (2006) *Multiple intelligences; New horizons*. New York; Basic Books.

Haldimann M and Hollington A (2004) *Effective learning support in international schools*, Effective international schools series, ECIS. Saxmundham: Peridot Press.

Hayden M and Thompson, J (2011) Teachers for the international school of the future, in R

Bates (ed), *Schooling internationally; Globalisation, internationalisation and the future for international schools.* Abingdon: Routledge [94-111].

Lawrence, J (2009) Pupil behaviour and teaching strategies, in S Younie, S Capel and M Leask (eds), *A handbook for higher level teaching assistants.* Abingdon: Routledge [60-81].

Oliver, R (2004) Writing 'in your own words': Children's use of information sources in research projects, in G Rijlaarsdam, H Van den Bergh and M Couzijn (eds) *Effective learning and teaching of writing: A handbook of writing in education* (2nd edition). New York: Kluwer Academic Publishers [367-380].

Rose, R and Forlin, C (2010) Impact of training on change in practice for education assistants in a group of international private schools in Hong Kong. *International Journal of Inclusive Education*, 14 (3) 309–323.

Tarry, E (2011) British international schools; The deployment and training of teaching assistants. *Journal of Research in International Education*, 10 (3) 293–302.

Walton, A and Goddard, G (2009) *Supporting every child; A course book for foundation degrees in teaching and supporting learning* (Teaching Assistants' Handbooks). Exeter: Learning Matters.

Whitehorn, T (2010) School support staff topic paper. Schools Analysis and Research Division. Nottingham: Department for Education.

Chapter 11

The IPC: children's perspectives in an English state school

Mary van der Heijden

Introduction

Early in this millennium, changes took place in the national state-funded education system of England that gave individual schools greater autonomy over their choice of curriculum. The published framework *Excellence and Enjoyment* (DCSF, 2003) states: 'We want schools to take ownership of the curriculum, shaping it and making it their own. Teachers have much more freedom than they often realise to design the timetable and decide what and how they teach' (p3). Schools were thus given the impetus to develop their pedagogy, to extend children's experiences and to adapt their approach and curriculum to fit best their particular circumstances. The government document went on to suggest that schools 'take a fresh look at their curriculum, their timetable and the organisation of the school day and week, and think actively about how they would like to develop and enrich the experience they offer their children' (DCSF, 2003: 9).

After being involved in international schools and international education for some years, on returning to the UK I became more involved in the English school state system. At that time many schools continued to use the government's schemes of work, but a number of schools had taken advantage of the change in policy and ventured to look further at their curriculum, both in terms of content and in the process of the delivery. One of the curricula available was the International Primary Curriculum (IPC) and some schools had incorporated this into their existing practice. Knowing the IPC as a headteacher, trainer and writer, this seemed an ideal opportunity for me to research what was happening within schools in England, particularly in the absence at that time of any published research on the IPC. The number of schools implementing the IPC in England had grown from 10 in 2003 to 398 at the commencement of my research in 2008, demonstrating a clear growth in the use of IPC in English state schools.

The government's decision to broaden choices for schools seemed likely to have contributed to this increase. Additionally, for some schools, changes in demography, international interdependence and the use of technology had an impact on their systems and curriculum content. Access to information about world events, including conflicts, has increased through technology. The need for immediate recognition, assimilation and understanding of events in the world, and to make sense of these events, is increasingly important to children as well as to adults. As schools have become more diverse, the need to change curriculum content and the way children are learning has not been confined to international schools, but is also apparent in national schools worldwide. Haywood (2002) notes that 'there is extensive interest in international education from institutions that operate exclusively within national systems' (p172).

Sylvester (1998: 186) cites Hayden and Thompson's five core 'universals' of international education:

- Diversity in student cultures
- Teachers as exemplars of 'international-mindedness'
- Exposure to others of different cultures outside the school
- A balanced formal curriculum
- A management regime value-consistent with institutional philosophy

Considering these universals in a national school context, such as the one that acted as the context for the research described in this chapter, suggests that national as well as international schools may provide an international education. One of the key goals of the IPC is to develop an international mindset in children by making the curriculum meaningful to teachers and children within their local context – whether that is in a national or an international school.

In recent debate concerning the definition of international education, there has been a development of the notion of 'international-mindedness'. Gellar (2002) proposed that for (international) schools to be internationally minded, they need two aspects. One is the curriculum that the school follows, and the second is what he describes as 'universal values' (p32), which he relates to peace, empathy and compassion – attributes that are perhaps difficult to apply to young children. Similar concepts to international-mindedness have also been defined, such as Heyward's (2002) 'intercultural literacy'. I was drawn to the notion of intercultural literacy as it seems a practical, viable way of establishing the development of the ability to 'read' another culture as an increasingly important skill in the modern world.

Skelton (2002) suggests that young children are egocentric and do not see themselves as part of the outside world: indeed very young children are incapable of even seeing themselves as themselves, and therefore cannot see themselves as part of the wider context. Skelton discusses international-mindedness as a continuum developing from the 'child' to the 'other': when we have reached an understanding of the 'other', we can be considered to be internationally-minded, a process that Skelton contends is slow and complex. Holmes (1995) would agree. Although Holmes states that the child can see him/herself as separate from others, he argues that the development of the self is complex, and he cites, *inter alia*, Spencer (1988) who suggests that it also 'includes acquisition of gender/racial identities' (p47).

My interest in the notion of children being able to look at the world from another perspective led me to the field of child psychology, and the notion of a developmental continuum of perspectives that would begin with an 'egocentric perspective', moving towards the child's realisation that others may have the same perspective, to seeing him/herself from another's perspective and being

Stage 0 Egocentric Perspective The child does not distinguish his own perspective from that of others or recognize that another person may interpret experiences differently.
Stage 1 Differentiated Perspective The child realizes that she and others may have either the same or a different perspective.
Stage 2 Reciprocal Perspective Because the child can see himself from another's perspective and knows the other person can do the same thing, he can anticipate and consider another's thoughts and feelings.
Stage 3 Mutual Perspectives Now the child can view her own perspective, a peer's perspective, and their shared, or mutual, perspective from the viewpoint of a third person.
Stage 4 Societal or In Depth Perspectives Children (and adults) can see networks of perspectives, such as societal, republican, or African American point of view.

Table 1: Abbreviated continuum of children's development of perspective (Selman, 1980; Selman and Byrne, 1974; Selman and Jacquette, 1978; all in Parke and Gauvin, 2008: 294)

able to anticipate and consider another's thoughts and feelings (Selman, 1980; Selman and Byrne, 1974; Selman and Jacquette, 1978; all in Parke and Gauvin, 2008: 294). The continuum summarised in Table 1 suggests to me that being internationally-minded is largely about being able to take on other perspectives and having the ability to understand the 'other'. This point will be further explored later in the chapter.

The IPC was initially developed for international schools with students from many regions of the world who were mostly what we have come to know as 'third culture kids' (Pollock and Van Reken, 2001): those children who have spent their formative years outside their own and their parents' culture. Drennen (2002) states that 'developing an understanding of culture is critical in promoting an understanding of others and an ability to relate co-operatively with them' (p61). This is clearly one aspect of becoming internationally-minded and children need to be provided with regular opportunities to develop this understanding. Drennen also proposes that 'developing an understanding of the nature and value of one's own culture is a fundamental starting point for any educational programme claiming to be international' (2002: 60). The IPC reinforces the view that an understanding of one's own culture is equally as important as understanding others through the concepts of 'home country and host country'. My interest in the child's perspective, and in the notion of home country and host country, led me to undertake a small-scale piece of research with children who had lived mostly in England and attended state-funded schools.

The research

This chapter documents the empirical research findings from a small-scale case study undertaken in an English state school, with the intention of contributing to understanding of the extent to which the IPC may have affected children's perceptions of the notion of being 'international'. The key area of interest was the international element of the IPC, which has specific and explicit international learning goals – reputedly unique to the IPC. This notion of being 'international' inspired me to research the meaning of the term for primary-aged children located in a non-international setting. The IPC states the following as an introduction to its international goals:

> The international goals are based on an understanding of the characteristics of an international curriculum. An international curriculum should develop in children:
>
> - knowledge and understanding beyond that related to their own nationality
> - an understanding of the independence and interdependence of peoples, countries and cultures
>
> It should enable children to develop both a national and an international perspective.
>
> (IPC, 2012)

In selecting a school in which to undertake my research, I felt it was important to find a school that had been using the IPC for more than two years so as to ensure that the children were familiar with the IPC terminology, and that they had experienced a variety of units from which to draw their responses. The primary school selected (which will be referred to here as School X to protect its anonymity) had been inspected and deemed a 'Good' school by Ofsted (Office for Standards in Education), the national inspection system in England.

Evidence from the most recent (2001) census of the population in the location of the school indicated that it was one of the least ethnically diverse cities in the area. While the region remained predominantly white British, over the previous three years there had, however, been an increase in the number of residents of Asian ethnicity and there was also a small population of Portuguese residents.

Interviews	Materials
Interview One **12 children from Year 4 and 12 children from Year 6** The children chose from a set of photographs. They were asked to imagine that they had met these children for the first time. They were then asked to write down the types of questions that they would want to ask the children in the photograph. Then they were asked to write questions that the children in the photograph would ask them if they met them. They could work independently or with a partner.	Each child was presented with a set of photographs from nine different countries across all continents. They also had an A4 sheet with two parts: • 'Questions I will ask the children' • 'Questions they will ask me'
Interview Two **10 children from Year 4 and 10 children from Year 6** The children were asked to think about an international person. They were asked to imagine what an international person might be like. They were given this question prompt: What would someone look like, say, do and behave like, if they knew about and understood other cultures?	One A4 sheet with one question. Each child had their own sheet of paper, but no restrictions were made on working with a partner.
Interview Three **10 children from Year 4 and 10 children from Year 6** Semi-structured interview centred around five main questions. Children sat in a semi-circle.	Dictaphone used to record and notes taken. Transcripts written.

Table 2: Research design

Two age groups were chosen for the research: Year 4 (8 to 9-year-olds) and Year 6 (10 to 11-year-olds). These age ranges coincide with the end of an IPC milepost (a two-year span of learning) and it was felt that children of this age group could best cope with being interviewed by me as a stranger. The spread of ethnicities in these two-year groups was typical of the school overall: largely white British, with some other white and Asian children – quite different from the multicultural make-up of many international school classrooms around the world.

The basis for the research was three interviews conducted using different approaches as summarised in Table 2.

One reason for selecting a case study as the research approach was to keep the children in a 'natural' environment with a child-centred approach to the research design. Not removing them from school would keep them in a familiar setting, with familiar approaches. This meant that the children would be challenged on their thinking, rather than be concerned and possibly distracted by being in a different environment and working in a different way to normal classroom work.

The IPC provides opportunities for children to give responses in their preferred way, which is linked to the concept of multiple intelligences (Gardner, 1993). By using open-ended questions, the research was exploratory and provided opportunities for children to give their responses at different times in different ways, such as drawing, talking and role-playing/simulation.

Interview 1: considering 'the other'

The first interview involved children in a semi role-play situation, where they were asked to write responses to a collection of photographs that depicted children in nine different settings: in Afghanistan, the Arctic, Ghana, Japan, India, Myanmar, Nigeria, USA and Tibet. Images included a mix of dress, including national costume, daily wear, 'smart' clothes and school uniform. All the photographs were taken outdoors in varying weather conditions, a range of socio-economic situations were represented and no adults were depicted. The rationale for the use of role-play was to establish if the children already had a sense of the 'other'; that is, if they could connect and see themselves from another's perspective.

Twelve Year 4 children and 12 Year 6 children were asked to choose one of the nine photographs that most interested them and to imagine that they were meeting the children in the photographs. They were then asked to decide what questions they would ask the children and what questions they thought the children would in return ask them. Both sets of children responded with similar themes, relating their question choices to topics such as home, school and general social aspects of a child's life, as can be seen in Table 3.

The Year 4 questions tended to be more direct and formed as closed questions, as shown in Figure 1, which is typical of the Year 4 children's questions. These are general questions that could apply to most children in the world.

Year 6 children, meanwhile, tended to ask more open questions that could not be categorised as they asked for opinions rather than facts. One boy, for instance, asked the questions:

'What is it like to live in the snow consistently?'

'What do you think of the world?'

Topics selected	Questions I will ask the children		Questions they will ask me	
	Year 4	Year 6	Year 4	Year 6
Language	3	0	2	0
Name	3	3	4	2
Age/birthday	11	1	8	0
Friendships	8	0	1	0
Family	4	6	1	0
Country specific	12	4	10	6
Religion	3	0	1	0
Feelings	1	4	1	1
Food	5	0	4	1
Games	4	1	3	2
Activities/hobby	6	0	7	8
School	3	5	2	2
Country – general	1	6	0	2
Favourite shop	2	0	2	0
Christmas	2	0	0	0
Holiday	1	0	0	0
Favourite pets	1	1	2	1
Favourite animals	1	0	2	0
Road/home	3	5	2	3
Sweets/chocolate	5	0	3	0
Rich/poor	1	3	0	1
Door	0	0	2	0
Favourite colour	0	0	1	0
Favourite school subject	0	0	1	0

Table 3: Topics of questions Year 4 and Year 6 children would ask children in photographs, and of questions they think children in photographs would ask them

'If you could live anywhere where would you live?'

'What would your dream holiday be?'

Interestingly, the questions that the same boy thought the children would ask him showed a marked difference and became more factual and specific:

Where are you in the world?

What language do you speak?

What religion are you?

What school do you go to?

Who is your best friend?

What's your favourite food?

Is it hot in your country or cold?

How old are you?

When's your birthday?

Do you like chocolate?

Do you like fun activities?

Figure 1: Questions I will ask the children (Year 4)

'What is it like to live in England?'

'What are your hobbies?'

'What are the houses like in Britain?'

'Do you have snow in England?'

Other Year 6 children also wrote questions relating to emotions, including:

'Why are you smiling?'

'Are you happy where you live?'

'Have you had a war in your country?'

Another child asked: 'Has anything tragic happened to you?'

This was an interesting question as it was in response to the photograph of the children from the USA, who all looked happy, well-nourished and well-dressed.

The variety of questions seen in Figure 2 shows the ability to contextualise the questions, both for the person 'speaking' and for the one being 'spoken' to.

Year 6 children also asked for more detail about where the children lived, in questions such as 'Do you live in small accommodation?' and 'Do you live in snow all the time?' In addition, children of this age group phrased their questions more often around feelings, by asking questions including:

'How do you like your school and would you like to change anything?'

'What do you like about your country?'

'How do you feel about your country?'

Questions I will ask the children:

Do you like it there?

Are you moving to a different country?

Why are you wearing that funny hat?

Where did you get it?

Did your granny knit that jumper for you?

Is it cold there?

Where are your parents?

Where do you like?

Questions the children will ask me:

What's your name?

What games do you play?

What is the highest temperature in your country?

Do any of you wear glasses?

What sort of clothes do you wear?

What do you want to be when you're older?

What school do you go to?

What are your houses made of?

Figure 2: Questions I will ask the children, and questions they will ask me (Year 6)

Another Year 6 child wrote:

'Do you like living where you are?'

'It looks like you are happy. Why?'

These questions could, of course, reflect the child's level of maturity of language rather than a wish to create a deeper understanding of someone from a different culture. However, these kinds of questions suggest that the older children seemed to want to know more than just the names of, or facts about, the children in their chosen pictures. Both year groups asked about activities, which would be a normal question to ask someone of a similar age, irrespective of their living conditions, country or situation.

None of the children appeared to see any significant difference between themselves and the children in the photos. The Year 4 boys, who chose the photographs with disabled boys in Japan, did not ask questions relating to a disability and did not mention it to me. It is also notable that food and sweets were important for the younger children, as might be the case for any group of children of this age, which could indicate that these groups of children would perceive the children in the photographs as friends and were accepting of them. We might presume that they understood that there are similarities in children's lives at a basic level.

Interestingly, the children did not display a great deal of geographical knowledge. At one point, for instance, a Year 6 girl described Africa as a country. This impression was fairly consistent throughout the research and, although factual knowledge was not a focus of the research, it was striking that the children made no reference to names of countries or regions. In my experience, an international school child would often make connections with, and references to, their own travels, and their home country or host country. The children in this school would not have that experience to connect to, and so seemed to base their questions around their own lives and experiences. They did not, at that point, make reference to learning experiences through IPC or otherwise. One might expect a child to reference a unit or piece of research that they had completed, but this was not the case.

In general, the children seemed open to different cultures when using the photographs to form their questions. The majority were able to imagine themselves from another perspective and to ask questions. There was no evidence to suggest that IPC was the sole contributing factor, and it is unlikely that it was. It would be unreasonable to make a judgement about the children's ability to perceive another's opinion, but the manner in which the children wrote their questions would suggest that, as they matured, they became better able to perceive that there are some differences and similarities with other children in the world. They seemed to acknowledge that there would be similarities in their lives, such as liking sweets and going to school, while at the same time being able to imagine differences such as, for instance, that the photographed children might have experienced a war (though there was no evidence of this in the photographs), or that they might have different ideas or impressions about the places in which they were living. The older children seemed to be quite sophisticated and mature in using open-ended questions, from which we might infer that the older children, with more experience, had had exposure to more complex situations and concepts than had the younger children. This point will be discussed further using data from the remaining two interviews.

Interview 2: children's descriptions of an international person

The second set of interviews involved the children writing or drawing a response to the following key question: 'What would someone look like, say, do and behave like, if they knew about and understood other cultures?'

This part of the research was specifically designed to target the notion of 'international', which is a complex word for young children. Given the lack of clarity evident in discussion on defining the concepts of international curriculum, international schools and international education in the adult world, it was clear that simply asking 'what is international?' or what is 'internationally-minded?' (despite this being a key component of the IPC) would be a fruitless question for these age groups. It was necessary to break the term down into language to which the children could relate. As noted previously, the IPC international learning goals expect children to be able to compare and contrast different cultures and countries. I chose to draw on this goal and to relate the question to a person the children might be able to think of and be able to describe. My motivation was that it might be easier for children to visualise someone they perceived as being international, and then to describe that person in their own words, than to respond in more general terms. Additionally, in IPC units opportunities are provided for children to give responses in their preferred way, linked with using their multiple intelligences (Gardner, 1993). The following guidance gave children a chance to consider an international person with a focus on visual, kinaesthetic, linguistic, interpersonal or intrapersonal preferences:

'Look like' allowed children to draw their idea of someone international, using visual ideas or prompts.

'Say' allowed children to think about the kinds of things international people might speak about, thereby addressing possible linguistic features of an international person.

'Behave' allowed children to think about any particular behaviour that an international person might display. A child aware of more interpersonal behaviour or attributes might highlight this area in their response. In addition they might consider more intrapersonal attributes.

'Do' allowed all the children to think of something they might have seen an international person actually do. This could be something personal, or an action they considered important for an internationally-minded person; again, I hoped this might allow more kinaesthetic children to highlight this attribute when developing their responses.

The depths of the responses were consistent with the previous (role-play) interview. Year 4 children tended to draw pictures that related to their own lives. For instance, one scene depicted children playing together outside in a playground and another showed children playing a football game. This response was centred on an argument about who would be allowed to play the game, and finishes with 'come on let's play' even though initially the figure is saying 'no'. This pattern was also seen in another scene, where the boys had defined an international person inviting another person to play football and the non-international person saying 'it's mine only they can play', implying that he was leaving someone out of the game. There is a sense that the children thought of conflict resolution and peace-making as elements of being internationally-minded. In the response shown in Figure 3, we can see

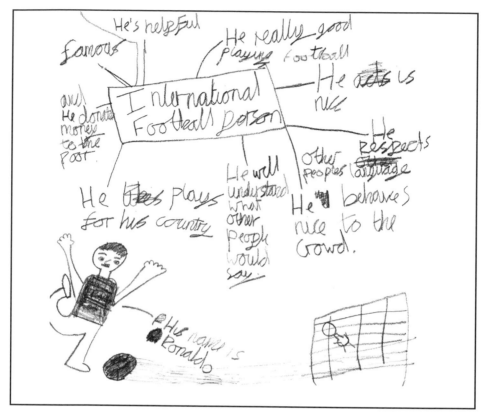

Figure 3: International Person (Year 4 boy)

that everything is again centred on the football game, the boy even mentioning 'Ronaldo'. Interestingly, the boy also notes that 'he donates money to the poor', 'he will understand what other people would say', 'he respects other people's language' and 'he is helpful'. The boys had chosen Ronaldo as someone they thought of as an international figure and they linked his attributes and behaviour to being 'international'.

The girls also drew pictures and cited 'sports' and 'eating well' as factors important for an international person, but they tended to emphasise the good behaviour of an international person, who would say 'my behaviour is good and I am always kind to people', and 'my hobby is being nice and helping people'. As seen in Figure 4, an international person would, according to these children, 'behave like a good person to a different culture', even suggesting that parents are responsible for showing them how to treat friends.

From these responses we could presume that children at this age perceive being international in a very positive light, where the actions of the international person are beneficial to others. They seem to have connected this point to their own lives, seemingly understanding that an international person should

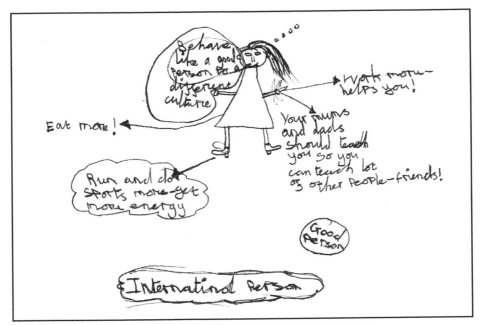

Figure 4: International Person (Year 4 girl)

have an impact on others, even if only in their immediate environment by, for instance, how they behave in a regular, everyday situation.

As might be expected, the responses of Year 6 children showed more sophistication in their language but also reflected more exposure and connection to the wider world. The majority did not draw a picture, but tended to create mind maps or to make lists. This way of working might also be influenced by the units of work, as creating mind maps is a regular feature of IPC 'recording' activities. The response shown in Figure 5 demonstrates a completely different set of concepts to draw upon as characteristics of an international person.

They may look like they're very multicultural.

They may understand that people behave in different ways to protect their country.

They would behave in a very mature manner.

They might talk about the fact that different cultures may do different things that you think are ludicrous but it is a way of life for them.

Their attitude might be different from what it was originally, from their experience of different cultures.

Figure 5: International Person (Year 6)

Figure 6: International Person (Year 6)

There is an aspect in these characteristics that demonstrates an awareness and understanding of the need to be tolerant in order to be international, although the precise word is not used. For this child to write that an international person would 'talk about the fact that different cultures may do different things that you think are ludicrous but it is a way of life for them' would suggest that they know about similarities and differences in cultures. This seems to illustrate their understanding that, while some aspects of a culture might seem alien to them, they should be accepting and tolerant of the differences. Another pair of children wrote in a similar vein, as seen in the graphic organiser shown in Figure 6.

The child draws out the ideas of being international in terms of defending beliefs; 'someone who will give up his life against right' and 'he should stand against torture'. These are not necessarily aspects that are explicitly taught in the units of the IPC. Through the more open-ended tasks in the IPC, however, children decide topics to research within a theme. For instance, in the unit Significant People (IPC unit Milepost 2) children may have researched the lives of people such as Mahatma Gandhi or Nelson Mandela.

There was further evidence that children viewed an international person as being associated with human rights or suffering, as illustrated in Figure 7.

A variety of responses dealt with deeper issues; one girl wrote that someone 'would feel the sorrow', another was concerned with not being 'racist' and that an international person 'would help the poor'. Whilst empathy and

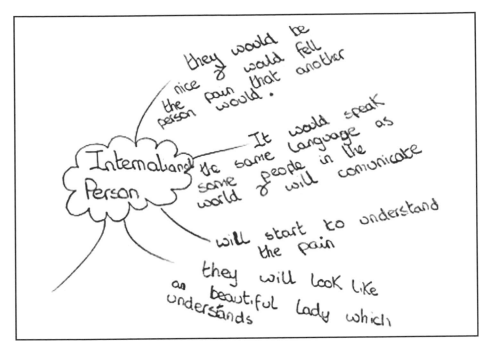

Figure 7: International Person (Year 6)

awareness of bias are not stated in these responses, they are implied in the descriptions. Racism, poverty and appreciation of religions appeared in a number of responses. Children had seemingly explored some of these issues, as there was consistency in the type of language they used. I would suggest that a national curriculum might not lend itself naturally to such topics, whereas these notions would be implicit in many of the IPC units. In the final set of interviews, children were asked for their views on specific areas of IPC linked with the international learning goals.

Interview 3: children's perceptions of the IPC

The rationale for including a semi-structured interview in the research was to record children's verbal responses to key questions, with a view to validating some responses from earlier interviews and to gaining an insight into their perceptions of the IPC. Five main questions were used in my interviews with both groups:

- Tell me about an IPC unit you have enjoyed.
- What did you learn most from the units?
- How are IPC lessons the same or different from other lessons?
- Why does the IPC ask children to compare different countries and cultures?
- Why is it important to understand about other cultures and countries?

The questions were used in the same order for both groups, but rephrased slightly as appropriate for the age of the children. They served as the basis for further questions arising from the children's responses.

In both year groups children seemed at first to confuse the content of IPC with literacy lessons, and the Year 4 children related IPC to use of the computer. They did not appear to know what was specifically an IPC unit. After some prompting the Year 4 children were able to talk about what they did in the Chocolate, Treasure and Healthy Living units. With a thematic approach it is likely that clear divisions between subjects are not obvious to the children. This seemed to demonstrate that the school adhered to an integrated approach and did not identify a particular IPC time. Interestingly, whilst they were not able to articulate clearly the content of what they were learning, the Year 4 children commented on the methods of working as being different when working on the specific units mentioned, as illustrated by one child's comment that: "It's different 'cause when we do like RE or literacy we have to use paper but when we are on the keyboards we use the keyboard and clips." Another noted that: "It's better with partners 'cause if you can't think of stuff, they can help you."

When describing a unit they had enjoyed, Year 6 children also seemed to be confused by the content in a unit. One boy brought *Peter and the Wolf* into the conversation. On querying if that was an IPC unit, he said: "It was like words and music combined, I think." On being questioned about what they had learned, once the group had established that Inventions was part of an IPC unit, they were more articulate about the details of their learning from that unit, as shown by the following comments:

> "Inventions are really, really cool. … you wouldn't have the technology now so it would be like the Tudor times. Basically our everyday lifestyle would be in ruins."

> Another boy stated that: "Our lives would be different. There would be much technology? We'd still be in the Stone Age."

> While another girl stated that: "Like all the people who have diseases and their hearts don't work properly, like a pacemaker, which was invented a couple of hundred years ago, saves lots of people's lives."

When asked about the importance of understanding different cultures and countries, the Year 4 children talked about the fact that they might learn about another language, help poor people and learn about the differences in the way they played games. One child said: "They can help you play their way and you can help them play your way." This was consistent with the earlier interviews, in that the children focused on their own lives and behaviour and playing well in the playground, as a possible analogy to being 'international'. It would seem at this age that actual content, such as details about a country or culture, is not considered particularly relevant.

The Year 6 children tended to talk to each other and to clarify what another child said. One child even commented: "I think he ... (another child) should have a go, he's too quiet." They were quite remarkable in the way they encouraged one another to contribute and it became more like a conversation than an interview. One child said that in IPC they were required to "think outside the box". Another child then clarified this further: "In, like, philosophy you have to think really hard and I thought IPC is something like that."

This train of thought then continued further with another child, who said that:

> "I think that IPC sometimes ties in a little bit obviously with philosophy and either art and history, 'cause like we've been doing lately, designing all these inventions, like our dream invention and that would be like thinking about why it would benefit people and also how to draw it as well. And then like the one that we're doing now is a boat and this goes back in history, also like part of the IPC, as well, like throwing it all together."

In some of the initial discussion, Year 6 children associated IPC with social issues related to poverty, mixed with a charity the school supported. They seemed to see that they would study aspects associated with other countries in religious education classes, but then they 'tie the two together' as one girl noted. They gave an example of this with conflict situations and finding resolutions. Possibly the most enlightening aspect of the interview was the manner in which the children showed respect for each other, by listening to and responding to each other's input. An integral part of the IPC units is collaboration in pairs and groups to produce work, or to discuss learning. This expectation does appear to have had an impact on these particular groups of children in this school.

Conclusion

Evidence from working with this small group of children in an English school suggests that the IPC plays a role in both the school's philosophy and the development of children's international-mindedness. The children talked about the notion of being international in a mature way, despite not necessarily knowing where they had specifically learned about it. It is clear that there is much that children learn within a school context that is not explicit or even expected. As Blandford and Shaw point out, 'What pupils learn is in part what the school sets out to teach them but is also the result of what happens incidentally' (2001: 4). The study suggests that there is a development of children's thinking, from relating aspects to their own lives in Year 4, towards regarding the outside world in Year 6.

It is important to note that interviewing children is not an easy task, and that interpreting their responses needs to be done with caution. Although the same terminology was used with both sets of children, the way in which the children interpreted the instructions and questions could possibly have biased and altered the responses. However, the children seemed largely unfazed by me, as a stranger to their school context, and they worked very much in a style consistent with the pedagogy described in the IPC units. That is to say that both age groups worked in pairs, if they wished, took turns and listened to each other's suggestions. Organising the children in a familiar way and replicating the genre of activities the children would experience in IPC (using graphic organisers or diagrams, for instance) seemed to alleviate some potential problems such as not being able to elicit genuine responses from the children, one child dominating the group, or the children not being able to stay focused on the subject and task at hand. Children seemed to work as if they were in the classroom itself and, in particular, they appeared to be familiar with listening and responding to each other.

Ultimately listening to children's voices was an integral focus of this research. As pupil participation becomes an important part of our developing view of children, it seems both practical and, in my view, vital that we ask children for their opinions. Purcell-Gates (1995) pointed out that 'when shaping reforms and changing aspects of education, politicians have major input and occasionally teachers, but rarely if ever are the voices of children heard'. To continue to develop and to improve the IPC, consideration could be given to the voices of the children, both as consumers of the IPC and as a response to the children's rights.

IPC units are detailed in their content, yet what the children remembered most clearly in this study was that they worked in a different way during IPC time, rather than recalling many details or facts. Fennes and Hapgood (1997) suggest that 'it is not sufficient to read books about culture, to deal with the subject on a purely cognitive and intellectual level... It is also necessary to learn from and with people of other cultures' (p73). They suggest that by doing this, we learn about the culture of other people's everyday life and the basic forms of 'social behaviour and action' (p16). The children participating in this research did not necessarily have direct exposure to those of other cultures, but through the pedagogy suggested by IPC they were being exposed to different ways of thinking.

The evidence from this study suggests that these children, from a 'non-international' background, were thinking about quite complex international concepts. One way forward for the IPC, particularly for Milepost 3 children, might be to develop the unit content by creating more challenging, or even controversial, content. Placing more focus on philosophical areas of discussion, such as good versus evil and justice versus injustice, could be further embedded in some of the tasks. Bartlett (1998) makes a convincing point in suggesting that 'whether one considers the question of an international curriculum from a practical or from a philosophical standpoint, one conclusion is inescapable: such a curriculum must begin in the primary school. Skills, habits of mind, attitudes, a common knowledge base – these are not developed in the final two years, or even in the final years of a child's life in school' (p90). The ways in which children learn to think and work together are most important. Habits of mind seemed to be most influential according to this research, and surely this is what is needed for our future world. To be able to see another person's perspective, to think critically about a topic, opinion or idea is a necessary skill for the modern world. The children interviewed in this study were already being given opportunities to develop these skills through the tasks provided in IPC units. Cambridge (2011) argues that 'there is no real difference between international education and education in a national context' (p142) since, among other things, positive attitudes towards community service and global citizenship are encouraged in both. Children from Year 4 tended towards an egocentric perspective, while the Year 6 children demonstrated an awareness of engaging with the IPC, as one child said: "so it benefits society." Certainly the children in this school had a very open attitude towards learning from and with each other, and were interested in improving the world and situations of others less fortunate than themselves.

On a final note, it would be interesting and informative for further research to be undertaken, involving children's voices, as a means of comparing differences and similarities in schools across the world. Replicating similar elements to these in a larger number of schools, both national and international, would surely be a worthwhile project.

References

Bartlett, K (1998) International Curricula: More or Less Important at the Primary Level? In M Hayden and J Thompson (eds) *International Education, Principles and Practice*. London: Kogan Page.

Blandford, S and Shaw, M (2001) *Managing International Schools*. UK: Routledge Farmer.

Cambridge, J (2011) International Curriculum. In R Bates (ed) *Schooling Internationally, Globalisation, Internationalisation and the Future for International Schools*. Oxford: Routledge.

DCSF (2003) *Excellence and Enjoyment: A Strategy for Primary Schools*. Nottingham: DCSF publications.

Drennen, H (2002) Criteria for Curriculum Continuity in International Education. In M Hayden, J Thompson and G Walker (eds) *International Education in Practice*. London: Kogan Page.

Fennes, H and Hapgood, K (1997) *Intercultural Learning in the Classroom*. London: Cassell.

Gardner, H (1993) *Multiple Intelligences: The Theory in Practice*. USA: Basic Books.

Gellar, C (2002) International Education: A Commitment to Universal Values. In M Hayden, J Thompson and G Walker (eds) *International Education in Practice*. London: Kogan Page.

Hayden M C and Thompson J J (1996) Potential Difference: the driving force for international education. *International Schools Journal*, 16, 1, 46-57.

Haywood, T (2002) An International Dimension to Management and Leadership Skills for International Education. In M Hayden, J Thompson and G Walker (eds) *International Education in Practice*. London: Kogan Page.

Heyward, M (2002) From International to Intercultural: Redefining the International School for a Globalized World. *Journal of Research in International Education*, 1 (1) 9-33.

Holmes, R (1995) *How Young Children Perceive Race*. London: SAGE Publications.

International Primary Curriculum (2012) Available online at www.internationalprimarycurriculum.com (last accessed 8 June 2012).

Parke, R and Gauvin, M (2008) *Child Psychology: A Contemporary Viewpoint*, 7th edition. New York: McGraw Hill.

Pollock, D and Van Reken, R (2001) *Third Culture Kids, The Experience of Growing Up Among Worlds*. London: Nicholas Brealey Publishing.

Purcell-Gates, V (1995) *Other People's Words, The Cycle of Low Literacy*. Cambridge, Mass.: Harvard University Press.

Skelton, M (2002) Defining 'International' in an International Curriculum. In M Hayden, J Thompson and G Walker (eds) *International Education in Practice*. London: Kogan Page.

Spencer, M (1998) Self-concept development. In D Slaughter (ed) *Black Children and Poverty: A Developmental Perspective* (pp59-72). San Francisco: Jossey-Bass.

Sylvester, B (1998) Through the Lens of Diversity: Inclusive and Encapsulated School Missions. In M Hayden and J Thompson (eds) *International Education, Principles and Practice*. London: Kogan Page.

Part D

The IPC as an Agent for Change

Chapter 12

IPC accreditation: more than just a quality mark

Graeme Scott

Introduction

In this chapter, I aim to provide a practical and personal picture of the International Primary Curriculum (IPC) accreditation process that will hopefully offer some concrete advice to schools interested in this type of accreditation. I will briefly describe the purpose and process, examine some options that are open to schools, and explain the reasons behind the choices we made at my own school. I will also highlight some of the outcomes we expected to see, along with some major school improvement outcomes that were as surprising as they were effective. Finally I will discuss a combined accreditation model and its potential benefits (albeit in the absence of supporting evidence or research at this stage).

In 2009 the International School of The Hague (ISH) became the first school to be accredited by the IPC. The accreditation was judged to be at 'mastering' level, the highest possible on a scale of mastering, developing, and beginning. We were of course very proud of our achievement and it still remains a milepost in the school's growth and development. However, the most striking element of the process was not the accreditation itself. What happened to the school in the months and years following the accreditation demonstrated just how far we still needed to go before we could finally call ourselves a true learning-focused international school. A graph charting the school's improvement would show that the curve was much steeper *after* the accreditation than before. The accreditation therefore acted as a catalyst, highlighting and clarifying the school's strengths and weaknesses, and springboarding us on to further improvements and innovations. Not all of these were IPC-related, but they all served to enhance student learning.

The International School of The Hague first opened its doors for primary (elementary) students in 2003. The IPC was the curriculum selected by the school leadership. In addition, the school adopted what were then the national literacy and numeracy strategies, established in the late 1990s by the incoming UK government to improve standards in these areas. These strategies were adapted to suit the international nature of our students. Then, as now, fewer than 20% of our student population had English as their first language and a significant number spoke no English at all. In addition to class/homeroom teachers, specialist teachers for music and physical education were employed, with their curriculum covering the IPC learning goals for each area with additional, subject-specific learning objectives. Dutch lessons were also provided to meet Ministry of Education guidelines and to help children better to integrate in the host country. In May 2012 ISH had around 550 primary age students from over 70 different nationalities, with a range of 60 languages between them. The majority of students are transient, staying at the school for an average of around three years.

The road to accreditation began for us in 2008, only a few months after the IPC announced the commencement of its accreditation programme, which includes a self-review stage. As a school, we had examined other accreditation possibilities and found potential benefits with all of them. A rigorous self-review provides school leadership with a range of quality indicators and an evidence-based mandate for change. But it can also provide a sharper focus in key areas of the school's operation. The school leadership team at ISH consulted key stakeholders and spoke with other schools and accreditation agencies before deciding that our drive to be a true learning-focused school should override all other considerations. We therefore wanted a form of accreditation that would focus on all different aspects of student learning and, at this stage, perhaps not much else.

The purpose of IPC accreditation

According to IPC, the purposes of IPC self-review and accreditation are to enable schools to:

- review their implementation of the IPC and its impact on learning
- implement the key elements of the IPC that most impact on learning
- make decisions about developments they need to make to improve the contribution the IPC makes to learning
- receive, when they request it, an external view of the school's own review and, when schools choose, for the IPC to award an externally validated mark of quality to the school

(IPC Self-Review Process)

This seemed to be a good fit in terms of what we were trying to achieve and the direction in which we wanted to take our school. In addition, the quality statement that IPC accreditation would give our school, though perhaps not the most important outcome of the process, would act as a valuable marketing tool. With a number of quality international schools in the city and a relatively tight budget, it was important for us to be able to reach a critical mass of student numbers and to demonstrate that we were providing high-quality learning experiences, supporting with externally validated evidence the positive stories we were telling in our admissions department. In addition, we wanted to be able to attract the very best teachers and knew that we could not do this through creating ultra-attractive salary packages. Our school is technically a state school, with salaries pegged to the Dutch state system and therefore not comparable with the best international school salaries. Perhaps we could attract great teachers based on the quality and reputation of the school alone? The decision was therefore taken to approach the IPC and to begin the accreditation process.

Self-review with or without accreditation?

One option open to schools is to complete the IPC self-review process only, without accreditation. High standards and expectations can be set by the school itself, followed by a thorough self-evaluation of where the school stands with respect to each of the rubrics. However, I would argue that the actual experience of the accreditation process provides an invaluable perspective that is not provided by self-review alone. I would also suggest that it may be more effective to be externally accredited at 'developing' level, than to self assess one's school as being at 'mastering' level. Part of our role as headteachers is self-promotion (of our schools, not ourselves!) and marketing. No matter how objective we are, we can always be – and should always be – proud of our schools and even emotionally attached to them. But emotional attachment and objectivity do not always sit together comfortably. It is easy to view our own schools through rose-tinted lenses, no matter how hard we try not to. An accreditation visit by professionals who are not linked to, nor employed by, the school can provide the impartiality and perspective that school leadership and staff may not. Self-review and accreditation can be two complementary processes that combine to create an accurate and valid assessment for the school's development.

In his paper, 'The value of external evaluation to schools' self-assessment', Heikki K. Lyytinen, former Secretary General of the Finnish Education Evaluation Council and author, educator and school inspector, outlines the strengths and weaknesses of self-assessment as follows:

The central strengths of self-assessment can be listed as follows:

- Effectiveness, as it involves personal and independent decisions, and because it is about activating, grass-root level practice. The information yielded is fairly easy to put into good use.
- Continuity, as it makes up a natural part of operations planning and the regular course of events. Very useful for formative purposes.
- Learning effect, as it is essentially about an intellectual exercise on experience, and learning from it.
- Characteristics of personal responsibility, which reinforces commitment.
- Flexibility and precision, as it can be tailored and targeted according to the specific needs and prior knowledge of the community.

- Information production, which serves various needs of school development and management.

The weak points of self-assessment are as follows:

- It is fettered by the system of social relations within the work community, so that taking a due distance from the evaluation targets may be more difficult.
- Subjectivity and narrow viewpoints, particularly in contexts where no comparative information is available.
- Emphasis on the positive characteristics and identity of the work community, so that critical views become more difficult to take. People prefer to see things in a positive light, because negativity increases anxiety within the work community.
- Inadequacies in the evaluation thinking and capacity of the work community. Evaluation skills can only be learnt through practice.

(Lyytinen, 1998)

Where self-assessment and external validation or accreditation work best is when the weaknesses of one are complemented by the strengths of the other. I believe the school's intimate knowledge of its students, stakeholders and unique situation can combine with the objectivity and clear success criteria provided by the accreditation process to produce a highly effective and accurate picture of the school's performance and progress.

Before arranging for the visit of an accreditation team, schools undertake a self-study based on the nine IPC accreditation rubrics. These are as shown in Figure 1:

A clear focus on children's learning

Shared outcomes about the kinds of children we are helping to develop

Awareness of classroom practices that help children develop as we would like

International-mindedness

An appropriate balance between knowledge, skills and reflection leading to understanding

Appropriately rigorous children's learning, and teachers' high expectations of it

Implementation of brain-friendly elements of the IPC

Implementation of themes through integrated yet separate subjects

Assessment and evaluation that supports and informs learning rather than dictates it

---

Figure 1: IPC accreditation rubrics (IPC Self-Review Process)

We chose to have a preliminary visit, which is not mandatory but rather an option that schools can call upon if they feel they need further information about the process. We had a number of issues that we needed to clarify in order to ensure we were on the right track. Some of the rubric statements were, in our view, ambiguous or at least a little unclear. In addition, my own view was that there was a danger that we had become too close to some of the sources of evidence that really mattered. We needed an objective, critical viewpoint from someone who had been part of the accreditation process from its inception. We did not have the option of consulting with another school as at that stage no other schools had gone through the accreditation process, so we called IPC and arranged a visit.

We went into this preliminary meeting armed with a number of questions. Howard Marshall from IPC provided the clarifications that we needed, but posed some questions of his own. The crucial question asked of us was whether we had an agreed definition of learning and, if so, if it was shared with the entire school population. Our answers were 'no' and, again, 'no!' We all knew that knowledge, skills and understanding were big players, but there existed no consistent and agreed definition across the school. Later in this chapter, I will show how important Howard's question was in our journey as a learning-focused school. Following his visit, we began to assemble our evidence, before booking a date for our accreditation visit.

Prior to the visit

The accreditation team do not have time while in school to sift through and select useful data whilst discarding less relevant information. Their time in school is very limited, so discussions between the accreditation team leader and headteacher before the visit need to be focused and unambiguous. Having too much evidence can be as problematic as having too little and can cloud the most important issues. Equally, anecdotal evidence should be avoided. Evidence needs to be clearly linked to the rubrics. For a more holistic school inspection, there may be the temptation to include all kinds of data. For IPC accreditation, if it does not relate to the rubrics, it should not be included. After all, the accreditation acts as a verification of the school's self-review and, as such, will not comment on anything lying outside of the rubrics.

The accreditation visit needs to be well choreographed in advance, with a timetable drawn up between the headteacher and the accreditation team leader. However, depending on what the team find (or perhaps do not find), this timetable can be changed and the focus may be narrowed down. The accreditation team leader writes to the headteacher to explain the format of the visit. At this stage the team are sent copies of the school's self-review, including judgments of where the school is in relation to the nine rubrics (*ie* at beginning, developing or mastering level) along with the supporting evidence. Various other agreements are made between the accreditation team leader and the headteacher before the final arrangements for the visit are planned in detail.

The visit

Our visit began with an introductory Monday morning meeting with staff. Each member of the accreditation team (in our case, three) gave a brief history of themselves and their career, and demonstrated that they had a grasp of what sort of school we were. As we are a strange cocktail of semi-public, state-sponsored international school with over 80 nationalities, understanding this context was important. A key message explained by the team at this time is that the purpose of their visit is to validate the school's self-review; it is not to inspect. The core purpose of the introductory meeting is thus to ensure that all staff are clear about the process in which they are about to take part.

Elements of the visit would normally include:

- classroom observations
- meeting with the headteacher
- meetings with teachers
- meetings with parents
- meetings with children

Our own experience at ISH suggests that all of these are valuable, but the classroom observations and meetings with children are perhaps the most illuminating and revealing elements. As children are the end users of the learning process, the evidence they provide is critical, and generally very honest and accurate. Many other elements of the rubrics may be in place, but if student learning is not happening at a sufficient rate and in appropriate depth, then accreditation is unlikely to result.

During the visit, the team examine a selection of documents relating to the nine rubrics. It is extremely difficult to group documents according to each rubric as there are so many areas that overlap. Due to the complexity of the learning process, many aspects are interlinked so one document may support two, three or even four different rubrics. Whenever a school chooses to go through an accreditation process, no matter how pleasant the accreditation team is and how respectful the process, it is an exhausting and potentially stressful time for the school. What made this sensation slightly easier for us was noticing how exhausting it was for the accreditation team too! This was clearly not a one-sided activity. It was a process done *with* the school and not merely *to* the school. This feeling was reinforced several times throughout the visit, but particularly through IPC's suggestion that members of the school leadership should accompany the accreditation team in classrooms, for observations. This was extremely valuable as it encouraged an atmosphere of transparency and trust. It also helped when feedback was given, as having seen the evidence ourselves we could relate better to the comments made by the team.

At the end of the visit, the accreditation team meet with the school leadership, which could be anything from the headteacher alone to a team of leadership and IPC colleagues. The purpose of this final meeting is to share some of the highlights of the visit, without revealing whether or not accreditation has been achieved.

After the visit

As soon as possible after the visit, the team leader drafts the team's report and sends it to the headteacher to check for clarity and accuracy. At this stage there is no mention of accreditation. Once the report has been returned by the headteacher, it is sent to Fieldwork and the team leader discusses and justifies the report with senior Fieldwork staff. The status of accreditation is then agreed upon, and the school informed soon after. Once we at ISH had heard the news that we had been accredited, and at mastering level too, there was a sense of satisfaction (and even euphoria) amongst the school community – but also a feeling of relief, as we knew from the final meeting that we would be fairly close to mastering level. After the event, we were careful not to misread 'mastering' as meaning 'mastered' and did not bask for too long in the glory of accreditation.

Since our accreditation, we have often compared the school to an Olympic athlete. An athlete can be a quality performer both before and after the Olympic Games, but will try to hit his or her peak of performance for the duration of the Games. In the same way, our school was a good school both before and after the accreditation, but we tried to show ourselves at our very best during the accreditation visit. However, I have since found this analogy to be only partly accurate, as our school is now far stronger than it was when it was accredited. I now like to adjust the analogy, thinking of our athlete as having employed a new and inspiring coach who, to quote Jim Collins in his book *Good to Great*, 'confronts the brutal facts' about current performance then focuses on a range of different strategies and a changed mindset (Collins, 2001). The way in which we addressed learning after the accreditation was very different. We revised the techniques we used to assess whether learning was happening in our classrooms, we refocused away from the teacher and teaching and more towards the learner and learning. The daily chat in the staffroom changed and became more learning-focused, though we still managed to maintain the staple conversational diet of shopping, shows and shoes! Much like an athlete's coach may change the way in which the athlete runs, jumps or throws, initially some of these changes can feel uncomfortable – but after a while, the successes they bring are clear, tangible and sustainable.

We had planned to construct a post-accreditation improvement plan that would prevent the sigh of relief at the end of the process turning into a performance dip. However, what occurred was something quite different, and it was not at all a deliberately planned policy. Accreditation sharpened our collective focus in each of the nine rubrics and consequently made them more accessible to us all. This new knowledge-building generated an interest in the rubrics that was not present beforehand, at least not at this level. Many of the teachers found their own individual passion in one or more of the rubrics; some staff even became passionate about assessment! The result was the creation of 'mini-experts' who found one area of expertise or interest, and worked alongside our IPC leader for learning and school leadership to develop this area. Although this suggests a piecemeal approach to development, what evolved was a much more corporate feel to the progress we were making. We branched off into sub-groups: some with a new-found fascination for brain research (rubric 7: Implementation of brain-friendly elements of the IPC), others on a mission to make our personal goals more tangible and meaningful to the children (rubric 2: Shared outcomes about the kinds of children we are trying to develop).

Now back to Howard Marshall's question about whether we had a clear and agreed definition of learning; when the question was first asked, we didn't. We had assumed that everyone knew what learning was all about. After all, we're teachers, so understanding learning should be a basic prerequisite, right? However, when we began discussing learning and what it meant to us, the range of opinions was staggering. We spent around two hours discussing the word 'understanding' and ended up more confused than when we started. We closed the school for a day and took staff on a residential trip to the centre of The Netherlands where we stayed, played and discussed well into the night. Only after that did we begin to approach a consensus. Now, several years on, we have a revised and regularly reviewed learning statement. It drives everything we do and is the focus of all school development activities. It is regularly communicated to parents and always shared with students, in English as well as in their own mother tongue. It has generated a lot of discussion, and the intellectual traffic that began to flow between my inbox and that of our parents was astonishing. Any little snippets about learning found in a wide variety of publications and papers were shared. Our newsletters became more learning-focused and shared recent educational research with our parents. Our teaching and learning policy morphed into a pure learning policy which focused on how to identify whether learning is happening, whether it is appropriate learning, and how to monitor these processes. It focuses less on teaching styles and strategies, and more on the conditions needed to create deep and meaningful learning.

In *Leading in a Culture of Change*, Michael Fullan argues that 'change cannot be managed. It can be understood and perhaps led, but it cannot be controlled' (Fullan, 2001). In our case, accreditation generated enthusiasm (not simply exhaustion as I had anticipated on my less optimistic days), and this took us in a different direction to the one we had planned. But it was a good direction and it was the direction in which the teachers wanted to go. It has generated much more ownership of IPC than before, and established a culture of support and knowledge-sharing. Since accreditation it has been much easier to bring new staff up to speed with IPC. Previously, our induction process included attendance at the IPC summer school which provided a solid foundation of knowledge, as well as a session with our leader for learning. We still continue with these activities, but it is now easier to cascade specific knowledge about different aspects of the nine rubrics in a less formal manner due to the expertise staff have developed post-accreditation.

Joint accreditation

A number of schools apply for IPC accreditation as well as accreditation by the Council of International Schools (CIS). Whilst IPC accreditation is focused purely on student learning and the factors that affect it, CIS accreditation is more holistic and concentrates on many different aspects of the school's operations. For schools choosing to apply for both IPC and CIS accreditation, however, the preparation and upheaval amongst staff can seem never-ending. IPC accreditation works on a three-year renewal cycle, while CIS lasts for five years. However, since September 2011, agreements made between the two parties mean it has become possible to undertake IPC and CIS accreditation at the same time. CIS already cooperates with the New England Association of Schools and Colleges (NEASC), Middle States Association of Colleges and Schools (MSA) and the Western Association of Schools and Colleges (WASC) in a similar way, leading to the possibility of dual accreditation.

The new CIS/IPC accreditation process uses a joint protocol, with an IPC section added as Section H of the CIS 8th edition Guide to School Evaluation and Self Evaluation (see below). For joint accreditation, the sections of the CIS self study have been restructured as follows:

Section A: School Guiding Statements

Section B: Teaching and Learning

Section C: Governance and Leadership

Section D: Faculty and Support Staff

Section E: Access to Teaching and Learning

Section F: School Culture and Partnerships for Learning

Section G: Operational Systems

Section H: IPC Criteria

CIS points out that:

the CIS Standards for Accreditation are designed to ensure that a school is offering an international education of high quality. The Standards contain many references to three 'Driving Ideas' which urge the school to be:

- Mission Driven and Vision Led (the importance of the school's own Guiding Statements)
- Heavily focused on Student Learning and Student Well-Being

- Committed to Internationalism/Inter-culturalism to foster Global Citizenship

(Council of International Schools, 2012)

When we compare the purpose of CIS accreditation and these 'driving ideas' with the IPC accreditation rubrics, the overlap is obvious, particularly in the area of student learning and international-mindedness. It could be argued that almost all policies, practices and procedures in schools will have a direct or indirect effect on student learning. At the time of writing, no schools have yet been through CIS and IPC joint accreditation. However, I believe these processes would support each other rather than contradict or conflict. Examining again the IPC rubrics, one can see how they would complement those in the CIS accreditation: they are certainly not two separate, disassociated processes. IPC accreditation is not a bolt-on extra. Although IPC team members will write section H of the report produced following joint accreditation, they will also make contributions to the following sections:

Section A: School Guiding Statements

Section B: Teaching and Learning

Section F: School Culture and Partnerships for Learning

as well as other sections if appropriate. CIS and IPC will be responsible for making their own decisions regarding the accreditation status of the school in question. The collaboration of two learning-centred organisations such as these may well, on the one hand, strengthen each individual accreditation process whilst, on the other, generating greater synergy between IPC and CIS.

Summary

The accreditation process drove us forward at ISH, but also gave us the tools to continue that drive ourselves. It marked the end of one process but the beginning of another, much more significant, quest for improvement. It celebrated what we had done well, but also set us on a more complex learning path where the depth and rigour of our thinking and our almost forensic examination of the learning process became a passion and a mission; a mission that we continue to enjoy sharing with our parent community and with – of course – our students.

References

Collins J (2001) *Good to Great: Why some companies make the leap, and others don't.* London: Random House.

Council of International Schools (CIS) (2012) Available online at www.cois.org (last accessed 22 May 2012).

Fullan M (2001) *Leading in a Culture of Change.* San Francisco: Jossey Bass.

IPC (no date) *IPC Self-Review Process.* London: International Primary Curriculum.

Lyytinen H K (1998) The Value of External Evaluation to Schools' Self-assessment, in H Jokinen and J Rushton (eds) *Changing Contexts of School Development – The Challenges to Evaluation and Assessment.* Jyväskylä: Finnish Institute for Educational Research, University of Jyväskylä.

Chapter 13

Quality and school reform: the role of the IPC in a school's DNA

Nicola Cooper, Catherine Copeland and Janet Harwood

Introduction

This chapter will consider the International Primary Curriculum (IPC) and its implementation and effectiveness at United World College Maastricht (UWC M) primary and pre-school over a 10-year period, during an evolutionary timeframe of school development from just after the new millennium to present day 2012. An analogy of the DNA double helix will be used to show how the IPC, as a strand of school development, has been instrumental as a change agent for grounding quality in our school reform efforts. The chapter will provide a case study of one school's experience through (in IPC terms) beginning, developing and mastering stages, and discuss both where the IPC and school development bonded in success and quality, and where they did not bind and modifications were thus made by the school. At some points in our evolution the management team felt that the school had superseded IPC in the course of our own development; that our own development had progressed in advance of the IPC. In the various sections of the chapter, and wrapped up in the conclusion, we will attempt to provide some insight into where the IPC curriculum was effective, where it was not, and how the IPC curriculum could consider extending development for the future.

Background

In the Netherlands, the Dutch government has established a number of schools to accommodate growing numbers of international expatriates. These schools are organised as departments of existing Dutch schools, known as 'international departments'. In describing the recent historical or evolutionary path of the development of the United World College Maastricht (UWC M) primary and pre-school, it has been helpful to use an analogy of a double helix from the common DNA model. The UWC M primary school's DNA was only recently formed in 2007, from the fusion of a Dutch international department school (Joppenhof International Department) and an international parent-run pre-school (Mosaic International Preschool). A secondary fusion occurred more recently with the formation of the UWC M in 2009, when these two entities merged with the International School Maastricht and the United

World Colleges (UWC), thus creating the 13th UWC worldwide. United World Colleges were established post-Second World War 'with the vision of bringing together young people, offering an educational experience based on shared learning, collaboration and understanding so that that the students would act as champions of peace' (UWC, 2012).

The UWC M primary and pre-school's genetic code is therefore made up of a number of entities to start with, but is further complicated by its family relationships; it has become a 'sister' to 13 Dutch international primary and secondary schools through its membership of the Dutch International Schools (DIS), the principal aim of which 'is to provide international children relocating to the Netherlands with such education that they are prepared optimally for either the transition to English language education abroad or a possible transition to full Dutch education' (Dutch International Schools, 2012). Moreover, UWC M primary and pre-school is governed by its 'mother', the local Dutch School Board MosaLira, which operates primary schools and pre-schools in the city of Maastricht. As a member of DIS, UWC M primary and pre-school is an international school funded publicly by the Dutch government. To supplement this government funding, the college charges relatively low parental tuition fees in order to increase the number of teachers and accommodate the specialised needs of running the international curriculum programmes. Thus the school operates in a public/private hybrid configuration. To further complicate this hybrid structure, the governance of the school is made up of three pillar members in a cooperative structure: the primary school board MosaLira, the secondary school board Stichting LVO, and the United World College Netherlands, together creating United World College Maastricht. The UWC M at present offers the IPC at primary level, with the International Baccalaureate (IB) Middle Years Programme (MYP) and IB Diploma programme offered in the secondary school.

Beginning

Our primary school created a link with the newly-founded IPC just after the start of the millennium – a time when 21st century learning was being redefined against the backdrop of the enormous global changes of the new knowledge society. Although only one of the three authors of this chapter was working at the school at this time, as the basis of this chapter we conducted a forensic study by tapping into our collective memory and digging up old documents to reflect on this period. According to these sources, the decision to use the IPC was made by the management of the time in response to pressure from the DIS schools to adopt either the IB Primary Years Programme (PYP) or the IPC for consistency across the Dutch International Primary Schools (DIPS). The original IPC presentation given by IPC directors and their colleagues was treated rather sceptically by some of our staff as being too commercial and simply 're-packaging' good practice, although the 'focus-on-learning' concept was felt to be interesting and worthwhile. Despite initial staff hesitation the curriculum was purchased, membership signed and the IPC framework was adopted to revolutionise learning in our school.

At that time in the school's almost 30-year history, the primary department had approximately 140 students and 12 staff members. The majority of students were English native speakers and the staff comprised a majority of Dutch native speakers with international experience, along with a third of English native speakers, mostly of British origin. It had operated using loosely defined topics following English curriculum objectives. The school had experienced a vast turnover of governance and leadership. It had become a member of the newly-formed school board MosaLira, which had trouble finding local directors who could understand and cope with the expectations, demands and levels of an international clientele and their specialised needs. The school board itself was also getting acquainted with operating an international school within their own national framework. The school's DNA at this time suffered from ill-prepared and changeable management, confusion of Dutch versus international culture and educational norms, discontinuity of curriculum provision and, most importantly, a lack of vision and mission. Its reputation was poor due to unrealistic comparisons with private international schools in Brussels, Bonn and worldwide. Parents were interfering with school operations, and communication, publications and identity were all very weak or even non-existent. Accountability and results were not communicated, nor were roles and responsibilities defined. Relationships within the school could be described as strained. The varying opinions, approaches, expectations and lack of leadership left staff, students and parents in a precarious and confused state of instability. An 'artificial shell', a superficial identity with little depth and clarity' could describe the primary school at that time.

With the introduction of the IPC, early staff meetings focused on trying the topics, purchasing resources, evaluations and responding to staff questions. Staff attended IPC workshops with a view to getting acquainted with the IPC. Discussions gradually turned to a focus on learning. Staff slowly became familiar with the format, content and vocabulary of the IPC programmes. Letters to parents involving them in the learning were appreciated and enthusiasm began to grow. The IPC started a kind of chain reaction effect whereby the chromosomes of the school DNA were becoming learning-focused, and this trickled into other areas of the curriculum. Our curriculum polymers were born as decisions about topics and content were made and a learning pathway was formed through setting the mileposts. This pathway gave a structural purpose, a sequence to follow and an initial framework for curriculum development in the school.

At that time our mathematics programme was aligned to a US framework under the leadership of an American headteacher. The language curriculum was produced in individual islands of traditional teaching under headings of reading, grammar, literacy, spelling, comprehension and phonics. Schemes were mostly used as the basis for curriculum. Attempts to change this toward a more modern approach were often met with resistance and even refusal. One of the essential cultural norms in The Netherlands is that most decisions are made through a consensus approach, and those that are not are not always abided by. In the context of unstable management, decision-making was often left to the discretion of the staff, which remained the only consistent factor during that period. This reinforced the consensus approach towards decision-making. One useful aspect of having a focus on learning was that it opened the way to reflection and evaluation on other areas of our curriculum. It provided a non-threatening reason to look at our practice and to have some necessary debates about where changes were needed.

By early 2005 strands were forming, though still far from of sufficient quality, when a number of dramatic events shook the school and led to a change in its path. Firstly, the first promising internationally-focused director (responsible for running of the school overall) suddenly passed away, and this was followed by the abrupt departure of the American headteacher (responsible specifically for the international department) – thus leaving a large gap in management. Secondly, a change in the local expatriate population brought sudden growth to the student numbers. Thirdly, the parent-led pre-school was taken over by our primary school and, lastly, the UWC initiative was introduced to the new management team and the MosaLira school board. However, with a few years of IPC under our belt and a strong relationship with the IPC organisation, we were ready to move from the beginning phase into the complexities of the developing phase.

Developing

At this stage we introduce our double helix model (see Figure 1) to help represent the process as we see it, especially in the developing and mastering stages. The left strand represents school development and the right strand IPC. The location where the strands cross and bind forms the grounding line of quality. The open oval shapes, which in 'DNA-speak' are called the 'backbone', shape the areas of our school development where we have varying degrees of binding the IPC and our own school initiatives. The horizontal trajectory lines represent this development, and are also referred to as 'base pairs' in a DNA structure. The areas of development are sequenced to represent the evolution of the school in time. The areas of development on the left side of the helix (for instance SEN, ICT) are school initiatives. The areas depicted on the right-hand side (for example, structure and framework) are a direct influence of the IPC. In some instances the bonds are not yet (fully) formed on one or either side; this represents a recent or future area for development. This image certainly reinforces the historical fact that the school started to reform at roughly the same time that the IPC came onto the market. In some instances the IPC has facilitated bonds and in others UWC M has had to find its own means of bonding to facilitate this development. Whichever force (school or IPC)

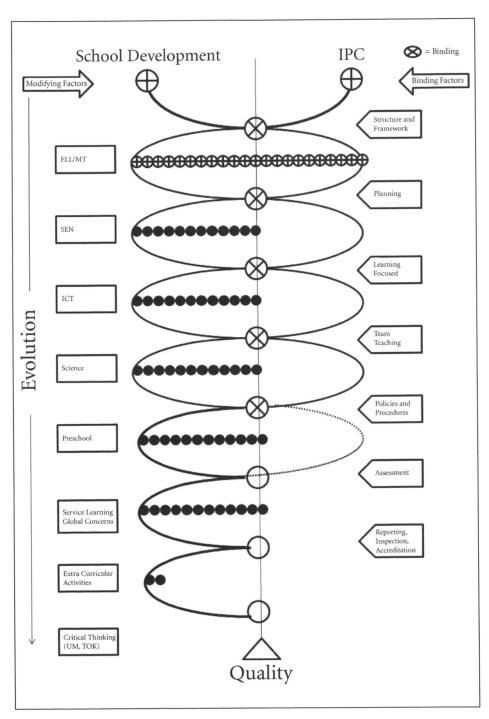

Figure 1: UWC M Double Helix Model

initiated the bond it is possible to state that the strong parallel relationship between school development and IPC implementation has been integral to creating stability within this evolutionary structure of school reform. More explanation of the development will follow in the next sections.

The new management team, consisting of a local Dutch director and a Canadian headteacher, formed the enthusiastic team that the school needed in order to forge ahead. The arrival of another 50 students in a school with little space brought about the idea of team teaching. Each year level shared a team of teachers who plan and teach the class with flexible groupings and differentiation. Additional specialist teachers were designated in the areas of Health and Wellness (H&W), Information Communication Technology (ICT) and IPC Science. These specialists added to an existing team of specialists in the areas of English Language of Learning (ELL), Dutch Language of Learning (DLL), Special Educational Needs (SEN) and Music.

Teacher coordinators were chosen to share leadership of curriculum and subject areas in language and mathematics and as the IPC Leader for Learning (LfL). The management at this time started to invest more in resources, staff development and their own learning. With the LfL, the director and headteacher attended an IPC leadership conference and reflected on how to develop learning further at the school. The majority of staff had opportunities to attend the IPC summer school or IPC training. The LfL and coordinator participated in creation of the rubrics for IPC accreditation which were then being developed by the IPC organisation, and these rubrics later formed the basis of our school initiatives for improvement and reflection. The structures and pairing of the chromosomes of the school's DNA were taking shape. Although this period was progressive, it was not without struggles. As the IPC grew, we grew alongside it. Frustrations arose with evaluations of the chosen IPC topics. Teachers felt that modifications related to age appropriateness of IPC curriculum content were necessary. The mileposts were thus shifted. Despite the frustrations we found a general groove, set the milepost topics, and things started to move along.

Management felt that the school needed an injection of modernisation and lacked the necessary IT resources to compete with other schools. Sponsorship was obtained to create a Dutch language-learning laboratory and to expand the English language-learning laboratory. This greatly enhanced the quality of learning in the modern languages area. With the school's vision in mind and availability of sponsorship monies, a short- and long-term ICT development plan was made, outlining immediate needs of the school on many levels of technological infusion. Through this, we acquired SMARTboards in every classroom and a computer laboratory. Each classroom also had stand-alone computers for student use. With the help of the ICT specialist, staff learned new methods and, despite the management team's fears, took up use of the technology with enthusiasm. This led to the subsequent decision to change the mathematics curriculum to the UK-based Abacus Evolve, which incorporated the SMARTboard in lessons and activities. Additionally, we initiated digital testing, assistive technology for learning difficulties, and teachers' planning done weekly by team teachers on the computer using a unified format, starting with learning objectives in each area.

We learned that one aspect of offering the IPC was the potential to become an accredited school, and we contemplated the possibility of putting ourselves forward for accreditation. In preparation, we consulted the IPC accreditation rubrics and learned that they asked for school mission and values, and the school's definition of learning. This task led to several IPC in-service days where we reflected on our definition of learning and came to decisions as to what it was. We also came to work on our student outcomes, which resulted in the development of a teaching and learning policy and an associated poster depicting our mission statement, as follows:

> At the UWC M Primary and Preschool, we define learning as an ongoing process of acquiring new and consolidating existing knowledge, skills and understanding. Through this we aim to develop emotionally intelligent and internationally minded world citizens. We want to help develop children who are resilient, cooperative, communicative, global minded, respectful, enquiring, thoughtful and adaptable and moral learners. (These are also our shared exit outcomes).

Our focus on learning reflection led to a decision to take on evidence-based assessment with student targets as a focus. We researched and developed student-led conferencing and student portfolio use. Simultaneously, management created an assessment box with samples of various ways to assess and provide evidence of learning. The box contained all kinds of materials including sample assessment forms, tracking tools, target sheets, observation notes, Post-it notes, clipboards, happy and sad face signs, and other easy ways for students to assess their own work and set their own targets, and for teachers to facilitate the assessment of learning. The box revealed a mirror when the lid was lifted, for self-reflection: something we wanted to encourage the staff to do. One year later, the IPC came out with its own version of an Assessment for Learning box. As we had already created our own, it was not something we invested in.

The biggest change to our DNA occurred with a change of the English Language Learning (ELL) programme. With growth in numbers, the majority of students were now coming to us with little or no English. The ELL programme had grown from involving a few students in every class to including a majority of our students; it now comprises 94% of the school population. We hired an additional teacher and implemented a two-level ELL programme to represent the differing levels of acquisition. Attempts to link the ELL programme with our curriculum were initiated, and our ELL staff began to research how to incorporate mother tongue support whilst still facilitating language acquisition and responding to the needs of our growing number of third culture kids (TCK). This resulted in a shift in approach towards language learning which considered three components as equally important factors of the same process: language acquisition phases, the importance and role of the mother tongue in this process, and the social and emotional needs of the children during a time of transition in their lives.

The ELL programme, through its topic-based approach, also created a much-needed link into the mainstream classroom through the IPC in the form of a focus on vocabulary related to the IPC topics. This was the second phase of the in-house-developed ELL Foundation Programme. The first phase initially focused on the acquisition of basic interpersonal communication skills (BICS) through survival topics to address the children's immediate language needs. Forming this bond between the ELL programme and IPC offered us an existing medium with which to further support our ELL students with the cognitive academic language proficiency (CALP) they were being expected to achieve in the classroom environment.

This approach was in line with current research and practice in the field of international education, and the school followed the developments of the ECIS English as a Second Language (ESL)/Mother Tongue (MT) committee. Parent workshops were established to promote and support parents with TCK and mother tongue maintenance. Staff embarked on the ESL in the Mainstream professional development training (Unlocking the World, 2012) and, in general, the school started to equip itself to accommodate the student population. As part of this initiative, a proposal was put to the IPC organisation in 2008 in an attempt to bring to the forefront the potential bond between ELL and IPC. A meeting took place between the UWC M ELL coordinator and IPC colleagues, though the proposal did not lead to any concrete outcome. We therefore developed our own school ELL foundation programme, connecting the base pairs ourselves.

In early 2006, the Mad Science group (Mad Science, 2012) arrived to lead a workshop for the whole school. The excitement and vibe they generated about science was fantastic. We allowed them to start an after-school club and run a summer camp at the school. Soon thereafter the management saw how Mad Science fuelled enthusiasm for science with the children. We did not see the same response within IPC science lessons, and we thus embarked on a relationship with Mad Science to link workshops to IPC topics as a means of injecting some excitement into the area of science in the school. Meetings were held with the newly-appointed IPC science coordinator, IPC coordinator and Mad Science to create workshops that complemented our IPC topics. As a result, one workshop continues to be held per topic for all of our IPC topics from pre-school to Year 6.

Taking over the Mosaic pre-school was a huge undertaking of significant importance to our international community. A new pre-school teacher was brought on board to professionalise the programme, and to assist management with creating policies and procedures to align the pre-school with the primary school programme. Our pre-schoolers start with several mornings a week at age two, and move to our primary school upon their fourth birthday. The pre-school programme operates a topic-based approach. At this early stage, the focus was on looking at how the programme could interact seamlessly in our community and operate under the umbrella of the primary school. The benefits of accessing specialists from primary and linking approaches such as ELL and DLL were explored and initiated, as well as opening access to other school programmes and facilities such as music, library and Mad Science.

As we worked towards becoming the 13th UWC worldwide, we became acquainted with the UWC movement's commitment to service and learning (S&L) as well as global concerns (GC). Coordinators were appointed for S&L and GC. They attended conferences to develop an S&L and GC programme in the primary school. A visit to our UWC sister school in Singapore injected much enthusiasm for the kind of projects that were possible. The practice of marking Peace Day and Earth Day at school was initiated and each year group started two projects, one focused within school and one outside of school. The natural link for these topics within the curriculum is IPC. For example, in the Chocolate unit the children focus on Fair Trade and the campaign for the use of Fair Trade products in our school and community.

Mastering

The biggest engineering feat in structuring our genetic code came in 2009 when we moved to temporary accommodation adjacent to our secondary school. This move established us as UWC M, and started a new alignment process which is still underway as we work towards a brand new campus due to be ready in 2013. In preparation for this move, the management structure was aligned at primary with secondary and brought about three new management roles. The headteacher became principal of UWC M primary and pre-school and was able to appoint two vice-principals, one focused on academics and one on administration and pastoral care. At the same time several new roles sharing the leadership were implemented to coordinate early years, lower school and upper school. With this shared leadership model the school launched its new identity and premises with many initiatives for quality. At this stage our numbers had grown to 230 students and another 30 pre-schoolers. Staff numbers had risen to approximately 40 (though not all full-time).

Early in 2009 the team solidified the school's IPC learning definition and policy. Policies and procedures were created and existing ones reviewed, with the school's learning policy as the central reference. New handbooks, website, welcome packs and materials were all created for our new identity as UWC M. Being a 'learning-focused' school remained at the forefront of every development at UWC M primary and pre-school. Team teaching has become one of the facets of our approach; an approach that was initially difficult and challenging to implement has shown its benefits to the learning process. Planning and meetings, shared leadership and a professional learning community are taking root and showing their worth.

One noticeable programme that was successfully implemented, after much trial and error, is our after-school extracurricular activities programme. In Dutch schools, it is not the norm to provide activities after school as the neighbourhood and community organisations provide many sports and cultural activities for children. In the effort to offer such opportunities for international children we started an after-school programme for personal development. The mission of the after-school programme is strongly linked to our IPC student outcomes. All kinds of lessons are offered for mother tongue languages, sports activities, creative pursuits and the like after school, and are given by staff, students from secondary, parents and local experts. These activities extend opportunities for our students to try all kinds of activities which might not otherwise be available, such as slacklining, expressive painting, karate, knitting, cooking, chess or Capoeira. Wherever possible, links are made to the IPC in content or philosophy.

Assessment has a number of facets at the college. We have a regular digital testing regimen that is implemented annually. It begins early in the school year when our Year 4, 5, and 6 students complete cognitive ability tests to set a baseline for performance over the year. New, non-English-speaking students are exempt from this process until they have been in-house for at least six months. Students usually complete this testing process in February. All students sit tests to measure progress in May to complete the testing cycle. In addition, on three occasions throughout the school year, language assessment for reading accuracy is implemented. All scores are reviewed by our SEN team, class teachers, specialists and management. Class discussions are held three times per year to share concerns about student progress and to develop action plans. Reporting is completed by means of two report cards. Students share learning goals and outcomes via student-led conferencing and portfolios, held biannually. Teacher observations and evidence-based progress are shared with parents during parent-teacher evenings. All in all, our approach to assessment, reporting and evaluation keeps the whole child in mind.

Data obtained from our assessment practices is tracked, examined, discussed, acted on if necessary and passed over to the next year class teachers. All testing scores are tallied across the school to focus on whole school results, with individual scores being noted and results questioned. From this, conclusions are derived and used to inform our planning and practice about resources, staffing and so on.

Through the development of the IPC as a framework in our curriculum, it was determined that it would be helpful if our reporting document were to emulate some of the IPC terminology. Consequently, the idea of using the IPC terms 'beginning, developing and mastering' was considered when redesigning our reporting tool. As a staff, we felt that a clearer picture of their child's progress would be provided for parents over the term if it had a similar phrasing style to that used in our IPC curriculum.

To help to explain the relationship with IPC and school development at the mastering level in the formation of our school's DNA, a few areas will be considered in more depth in the following sections.

ELL foundation programme

The aforementioned ELL programme continues to evolve. As a direct result of the recent postgraduate studies of our current ELL coordinator, the approach has become even more embedded in the socio-cultural philosophy underpinning language learning. The programme remains a two-tiered approach to differentiate between breakthrough/waystage (beginner) and threshold (independent) language proficiency students, as defined by the European Reference Framework (2012). The beginners receive four hours of withdrawal support per week, reduced to three lessons per week once the initial foundation programme has been implemented. These children then continue to receive ELL support with a focus on the IPC topic in their class. The second level is for children of threshold proficiency, who have one to two lessons per week to focus on the development of their reading and writing skills. Three specialist teachers support the implementation of this programme, with constant review and revision to keep in touch with the students' needs being fundamental to its success.

The ELL support programme at UWC M has remained one of the strongest features of our DNA identity since its initial development in 2003. One drawback of this strength is the perceived lack of a sense of collective responsibility towards language acquisition. Tentative steps are being made to address this balance through professional development, class discussions and subtle changes in terminology such as the change to using the term ELL, which suggests support as part of a process. Changes in attitude are being observed but such a school-initiated change in mindset is often gradual. If the IPC were to address this aspect and incorporate a language learning element into the topic objectives, this collective responsibility attitude towards language learning would be formally endorsed.

Mother tongue maintenance and the role of the mother tongue when acquiring a new language is no longer an approach isolated to the ELL department. The use of the mother tongue is a common approach in the classroom, where children are encouraged to refer to their mother tongue to support learning. Mother tongue maintenance lessons are encouraged and parental requests to establish lessons as part of the after-school extracurricular programme are facilitated.

Examples of successful base pairing

The most significant development has been the move to strengthen the relationship between English and Dutch language departments. This promotes the philosophy that the language learning process is common to both. To date the ELL and DLL coordinators have held regular discussions, worked with class teachers to develop a collective approach which reflects age and acquisition phases, attended the same language-focused conferences and trainings, developed a language learning handbook for parents, and developed a uniform report format influenced by a common assessment approach. The next step is to develop one school language policy in collaboration with the mainstream language curriculum coordinators.

The differentiated teaching approach to meet the children's language needs has also been implemented in the DLL department. There are now three specialist Dutch teachers who deliver lessons to the three stages of breakthrough/ waystage, threshold and proficient Dutch speakers. These same teachers have also been instrumental in developing the Dutch mother tongue maintenance after-school lessons. The DLL programme itself is a combination of current Dutch language programmes in conjunction with the IPC. If children are learning about volcanoes through the medium of English in their classroom, they will be learning about volcanoes during their Dutch lessons as well. This approach filters down to the pre-schoolers (our youngest students), who have ten minutes of Dutch-focused discussion every day where they talk about the weather and calendar (BICS) and then discuss their topic in Dutch (CALPS) with a plethora of Dutch songs to enrich the experience!

The language approach adopted at UWC M derives from keeping in touch with current practice and research whilst constantly monitoring and adapting to meet the language needs of the students. The IPC has clearly been used as a tool to facilitate this process; it remains, however, a school initiative. The IPC workshops offered at the IPC summer school to support teachers with the ELL/mother tongue aspect of teaching have proven useful to those who have attended, and the articles IPC has produced to promote language learning and mother tongue are informative. However, formalisation – through the addition of a multilingual, language learning element to the IPC topic objectives – would be a valuable and much welcome tool in the (inter)national schools' tool box.

IPC and ICT are naturally integrated together as IPC sets out learning targets that require investigation. Nowadays, this investigation is usually carried out using the internet. Basic ICT research skills are reinforced when students attempt to disseminate topics as presented in the IPC framework and gain greater understanding. One valuable aspect of how the IPC is organised is the fact that teachers can choose how to present topics and which elements they include in their curriculum delivery, dependent on the composition of the school community and their specific needs. This integration and development of skills in the area of ICT has included in-depth research, use of multimedia (including movies, videos and SMARTboard integration), and much more. The IPC has assisted in promoting 21st century learning skills at UWC M.

An important and notable aspect of IPC is that it presents itself as an age-specific curriculum, whereby all topics are relevant to the ages and stages for which they are intended. In the earlier milepost topics, students are challenged at their own ability levels. For example, students in Year 5 studying the topic The Brain used mind-mapping software to develop webs of brain functions. They discovered neurons, prefrontal lobes, the cerebellum, and their functions. Investigation of this topic facilitated the learning and implementation of the specific software, Inspiration.

A further example of IPC integration using ICT is the Year 6 topic, Feelings. As a culminating activity for the unit, teachers set up a Feelings Fair whereby students had to create a display representing their feelings. Students could choose their medium. Many chose traditional elements such as poster board or painting, but others chose to make clay figures and animate them in a movie to be presented on the SMARTboard. These same children embedded music and sound effects to help depict their message of emotion to the audience. The IPC allows our students to express themselves in a variety of ways, thus allowing the students to excel, gain technical skills, and show what they know.

Most recently, we have re-implemented the use of assistive technology in the school, whereby students with learning difficulties use specialised software and equipment to access the curriculum to a greater degree than would otherwise be possible. This programme was highly successful in the past and it is our hope that re-implementing it will allow more students to show what they know more readily. In addition, last month we introduced a trial in Year 6 using iPads. The goal of the implementation was to maximise the use of the learning tool to facilitate written expression, improve spelling, and allow easy access to research information for IPC topics. Feedback from the students and staff was positive, and they enjoyed the experience at the same time. Conclusions from the trial will be used to help inform our direction for future ICT use and deployment.

IPC facilitates inclusion. Our school is guided by the implementation of a Zorg Plan (care plan), which is government-mandated and assists us as staff to approach students with learning difficulties in a consistent, proactive and supportive way. In the execution of this schoolwide plan, teachers are mandated to accommodate and make modifications in curriculum expectations for students with special educational needs. The IPC is organised in a way that promotes flexibility for differentiation of topics at varying levels of student ability. Due to the fact that topics can be modified in the mode in which they are presented, teachers are able to include all students in the integration of the curricular expectations. As teachers approach performance tasks, students with special educational needs can be encouraged to participate in all possible ways. This may result in the modification of approach to a task, use or integration of specialised materials, or the reduction of expectations to facilitate success, but IPC makes it possible. This flexibility is embedded into the curriculum.

Repeatedly, our students with special educational needs voice their enjoyment of IPC topics because they are able to participate fully with their peers. They occasionally work in groups to investigate topics and are able to show what they know. This is most often a challenge for students with learning disabilities who may, for example, have difficulty expressing their thoughts in writing. In implementing the IPC, however, students have elasticity and choices built into their learning. When students work together on topics they share responsibilities, and act as peer coaches, encouraging each other to master the material. Students strive to meet performance objectives together, regardless of ability level.

The IPC uses a cross-curricular approach to meet curriculum objectives, meaning that all subject areas are integrated into the topic presentation. As a result, students are able to access the curriculum using their own particular strengths. For students with special educational needs, this is critical. Traditional curricular expectations limit how students are able to access curriculum, which, in turn, limits their potential for showing understanding. Historically, this resulted in frustration on the part of the student, and in student understanding being assessed at much lower levels. The approach of traditional curriculum has been very rigid and exclusionary. However, IPC has helped to facilitate student mastery of topic information using individual student abilities. For example, students with dyslexia might not be able to write successfully a 300-word summary of the topic Mission to Mars, but they would certainly have a chance to express their understanding of material by presenting a collage of the planets, their characteristics and the like. This elasticity of the curriculum is crucial for students with special needs to have the opportunity to realise their potential. The resulting confidence, self-esteem and self-assurance are indeed rewarding.

A new initiative: service and learning

Service and Learning (S&L) has become a real focal point within our college. The process of documenting S&L/IPC project planning is work in progress and will support our aim to become a centre of excellence in this field through the sharing of good practice. This aspect is also where the strongest bonds are being established between the primary and secondary schools. With the close collaboration of the S&L coordinators, a whole-school development plan and policy have now been generated. Again, this is a school initiative using the IPC structure as an existing foundation. Students from secondary are often to be found in primary, participating in and leading all kinds of projects. Class projects are running well and continue to develop. UWC M hosted a conference on service and learning in March 2012. A focus on water as a sustainable and renewable resource is an area where we are putting a spotlight through our curriculum. Linked to a science project where we hosted a science project fair, we are spotlighting water as a topic across the school and within the IPC topics to bring special attention to the issues surrounding water as a renewable resource. We are hoping that the IPC's recent collaboration with a water charity will strengthen our bonds.

IPC and the early years has been an area of concern for us. As we strive for alignment with our secondary counterparts in all areas (including curriculum, policies and procedures), one area that continually displayed a disparity was our pre-school. Because it had historically been parent-run, many aspects of its organisation had not been entirely consolidated when the pre-school joined the primary school. One such element was its curriculum. The new pre-school head has been able to implement many successful structural aspects. However, the basic curriculum remains unaligned with IPC. What we hope to do in our pre-school is to extend and expand the reach of the IPC to our youngest students: our two-year-olds. We feel that they are as immersed in our school as the other students; experiencing, feeling, participating, learning about international-mindedness, encountering other cultures, and all of the activities we have to offer. We are realistic, though, in recognising that these types of evolutionary pathways take time to establish. Pre-school staff are already providing an excellent service for our international community. This is definitely a next step in our development. Aligning our existing pre-school curriculum with IPC would bring further continuity to our educational provision.

Critical thinking skills are our most recent area of exploration. Our relationship with the University of Maastricht and their Problem Based Learning (PBL) model, along with greater links to the IB Diploma's Theory of Knowledge and MYP developments, have led to a strong interest in philosophy and conversations about the importance of critical thinking for young students. Our students display a pattern of high-level non-verbal ability, which may be enhanced by critical thinking activities. Of course, the relationship with the IPC will be part of this exploration.

Conclusion

As United World College Maastricht continues to strive for excellence and to engender 21st century learning skills in its students, so too will the application and development of the IPC continue in our primary and pre-school. As shown above, we have continually moulded the implementation of the IPC to suit the needs of our school community, our growth at the time, and our mission and vision. As these elements continue to grow, so too will our vision of how we integrate and execute the goals of the IPC curriculum.

The IPC curriculum developers are adding further components to the curriculum, expanding where possible. We are investigating how this curriculum meets our pre-school and primary school needs. Additionally we are looking at expanding its implementation at the early years level, seeking out ways in which to deliver this curriculum to children as young as two years old. We continue to adapt and modify the application of the IPC as we see fit to meet the needs of our school community. It is our intention to extend our programme of service and learning in order to be leaders in this field at the primary school level. ICT and service and learning are easily linked to IPC topic work and can be integrated into any school. The UWC M primary and pre-school advocates the encouragement of this thinking at an early age. We firmly believe that involving students and their parents in active service to others is important for the community of the future.

The two strands of IPC and school development at UWC M have supported each other in forming strong bonds of quality at UWC M. Some elements have been initiated by the school, and the IPC has offered a framework in which to place these initiatives and *vice versa*. This intertwining nature has embedded the IPC as an integral part of the school's identity. As we align and become a bigger school, new strands are being introduced into this existing helix; the 'UWC-ness' and the secondary IB objectives are but two key elements attempting to morph with the established bonds. It will be of interest to observe how this helix will evolve over time. Will there be genetic mutation or rejection, or will the DNA profile of the ultimate hybrid school finally be decoded? One thing is sure: the IPC remains an integral part of our genetic history, and one that will continue to imprint upon our school's DNA.

References

Dutch International Schools (2012) Available online at www.dutchinternationalschools.nl/ (last accessed 31 May 2012).

European Reference Framework (2012) Available online at www.coe.int (last accessed 31 May 2012).

Mad Science (2012) Available online at www.madscience.org (last accessed 31 May 2012).

Unlocking the World (2012) Available online at www.unlockingtheworld.com (last accessed 31 May 2012).

United World Colleges (2012) Available online at www.uwc.org (last accessed 31 May 2012).

Chapter 14

The IPC as a platform for change

Richard Mast

The context

My introduction to the IPC was at the time of my arrival as head at Stockholm International School (SIS). SIS had been one of the first IPC schools, and when I arrived it was fully operational and had a history of observable student learning. After reading through the curriculum documentation I was convinced that this was by far the best curriculum for primary-aged students that I had seen. A factor in drawing this conclusion was my belief that schools create enormous stress by spending too much time and effort in having teachers write curriculum. The assumption in this process is that teachers know how to write curriculum: analogous, to my mind, to assuming that all parents know how to write children's literature. This is clearly false, but we assume that teachers are experts in a writing genre that requires high levels of skill and understanding.

The IPC allows teachers to focus upon their core business: interpreting, implementing and then adjusting curriculum in light of the students they teach. It allows teachers to be educational practitioners. The curriculum presented by the IPC has several features that make this possible. The learning outcomes are clear and limited in number (and therefore practicable), and the pedagogy is articulated. Teachers can focus on what the students need to learn, and the pedagogy enhances high levels of engagement as well as allowing for the diversity of student abilities, needs and styles. Believing that the school's choice of the IPC was excellent, I spent considerable time in classes watching its implementation and the level of engagement of the students. The commitment level of all involved was high and the parents were very supportive of the approach used. In the three years I was there we monitored learning using a variety of tools, including international standardised testing and internal assessment defined by rubrics built upon the IPC learning targets. No matter how we looked at student progress, it was evident that students were able to learn effectively.

While in Stockholm, I was not convinced that the absence of reading, writing and mathematics from the IPC package was appropriate. This was very much a reflection of my belief that curriculum belongs to experts. In developing the IPC, Fieldwork Education could have built in these elements. The argument for the exclusion of mathematics, though, is stronger than that related to the core skills of literacy. Literacy is central to learning. Each school has its own view of how literacy should be developed, but this can be argued for any aspect of curriculum. For IPC to be most effective, it makes sense for the literacy to be developed and imbedded into the overall programme. Schools may not like to lose their autonomy, but there is a bigger issue here. IPC is designed to present a coherent educational experience for students. Leaving a central component to the individual schools creates a risk to integrity. If the IPC were able to identify a reading and writing model in terms of learning targets and its connectedness to the themes, then a major work element for schools would be removed. Once again we come back to the question of what teachers should do, rather than what they traditionally do or what schools assume they should do.

Three years ago I returned to China (having lived and taught there previously) to start a new international school. The choice of curriculum was easy. Fortunately, the development of the IPC as a worldwide, international curriculum meant that I could hire teachers already trained and experienced in the curriculum. I could also demonstrate to nervous parents that all would be well. The expansion of IPC to include early childhood was a bonus. It meant that students coming in at any age level were exposed to the processes of IPC and the associated strong learning experiences. The age-appropriateness of the curriculum is evident in the documentation and its implementation. What continues to be evident is that the IPC curriculum design allows teachers to recognise the support provided for best practice as well as being comfortable with its implementation. In the meantime, we have seen increased levels of learning and, more importantly, increased confidence of students in engaging in their learning. As a school we are still at an early stage but, with further training, support and experience, we know that our implementation of the curriculum will become even more effective. After six years of using the IPC, my confidence in its approach, philosophy and support structure is very high. Of course, one may speculate as to what needs to be improved in different areas, and how. Fine tuning discussions occur through the normal feedback mechanisms. In this chapter, I am interested in exploring four particular areas of the IPC.

Challenges and opportunities for the IPC

Defining primary education in a different way

The IPC is a strong curriculum. As such, it should continue to be refined in order to provide the flexibility required to ensure that the needs of individual students are accounted for – as well as allowing the unique personalities of teachers to be expressed. I am, however, continually mindful of one issue in relation to the purpose of the curriculum, which I would like to suggest changes over time as students develop as learners. Our long tradition has been to think of curriculum in terms of subjects. Though this is less so for primary than for secondary schools, the two terms are still intertwined. The purpose of the curriculum needs to be expressed upfront. For example, consider the learning needs of young students. For early childhood, the focus is on social interaction, all levels of awareness and the beginnings of literacy, numeracy and the use of an array of technologies. Subjects being taught here are reading, writing, listening and speaking, and mathematics. When we consider the presentation of IPC learning targets for the primary years, we see a reinforcement of the model of curriculum equating to subjects. There are targets for art, history and so on. Yet when we look carefully at what is being promoted, and certainly at what is desired, the focus is upon learning skills and processes. These are in the IPC as they are in most primary school curriculum models. The problem is that they are imbedded and implicit, rather than explicit.

Primary school teachers know that the core of their business is to ensure that each student is a strong and effective learner. That is why so much emphasis is placed on literacy as a foundation that enables students to access all aspects of learning. The skills required to be an effective learner begin in this phase of schooling. Many schools articulate this process as the development of the 'lifelong learner'. As such it is crucial. It is more important than focusing upon knowledge as it is all about how to learn, how to make sense of knowledge, how to research, how to study effectively and all the literacies (including those that are technology-based). If this is the essence of primary school education then it should be referred to as a curriculum. The IPC promotes and supports this approach, but maybe it should be brought more explicitly to the fore. If the learning processes and skills at an age-appropriate level were to be identified, and learning targets developed, then we would see formal recognition of what could currently be considered a 'hidden curriculum'.

There is another argument to consider here, which relates to the notion of integration. An integrated curriculum such as IPC promotes a recognisable and established approach. The themes provide vehicles for shaping the learning experience, for interacting with a wide range of knowledge and for developing skills and understandings. The aim is to provide for students the opportunity to make connections and to evaluate knowledge and situations from different perspectives. Critical in the process is that transferability of skills and knowledge should occur. Perhaps the real integration, if we are to accept the transferability argument, is much more about learning skills and processes. For example, a student needs to be able to research. This is a process requiring the development of skills and strategies and, as such, is a sequential process that includes reading of non-fiction text, and interpretation skills, as well as some form of synthesis to align the process to its purpose. The techniques and strategies for learning are available and well-researched, and the best teachers use them. However, an *ad hoc* approach is the norm for many schools.

What is really required is elevation to the level of learning processes being referred to as a curriculum, to have age-appropriate learning targets and with strategies standardised across the school. Students are too often exposed to different approaches to the same skills and processes. Many primary schools keep this in check to some extent through the class teacher spending a high proportion of time with students. Nevertheless, other teachers in the same grade level may use completely different approaches to the same skills (such as research, the use of bibliographies and so on). Different approaches can easily occur between grade levels. Students are then expected to use learning skills without schools establishing the curriculum, let alone coordinating its application. This is an area where IPC could take leadership. The core of this curriculum approach is already in place. The learning skills and the pedagogy for implementation are implicit in the IPC structure. The trick will be to identify learning targets and promote a set of strategies and techniques for schools to use. For example, which format the writing of a bibliography takes is not so important, as long as all students in school have the same approach in all learning areas. IPC would be doing schools a great service by adding this to their model.

The IPC and links with the IMYC

Fieldwork Education has recently engaged in the development of a middle school extension to the IPC: the International Middle Years Curriculum (IMYC). In general, middle school curriculum tends to be viewed as high school part 1. Currently, when primary school education ceases, from an organisational point of view students are placed into academic structures hardly differentiated from senior years of schooling. The curriculum is shaped, and defined, by subjects and the teaching and pedagogy reflects this new experience for students. Though there is a great deal of validity in this approach, there is often a failure to understand that the link with primary education needs to be honoured. If the core focus of primary education is to establish learning skills and processes, as promoted and supported by IPC, then it is important to consider what should happen in middle school.

Primary school teachers, particularly in Grades 4 and 5, are very aware of the dramatic change in learning approach that their students are likely to experience. They therefore tend to cram into their students' final two years as much as they can of the learning skills and processes curriculum. This is unfortunate as it detracts from the other elements of learning that are so important. Middle school ought to be seen as primary school part 2 in relation to learning skills. If this is understood and accepted, then the IMYC curriculum framework and implementation could be adjusted to give students the time to imbed their learning skills and to ensure that they all have the strategies of learning so crucial for academic success across the realm of subjects.

The IMYC is built upon the IPC structure, and is a logical extension that complements middle schooling. The integrity of academic subjects is not at risk. What is different from the IPC is that the learning processes continue to be developed and strengthened, as well as a significant emphasis being placed on higher order reasoning, logic and thinking. Themes are much broader and reflective of the maturity of students and, in addition, provide a strong foundation for pre-university learning expectations. A key difference between IPC and IMYC relates to its implementation. The IPC is largely the responsibility of one teacher. IMYC, meanwhile, is a shared responsibility. The themes provide guidance and direction for the development of knowledge, skills and understanding in relation to the expected content of subjects. What is not available as yet is provision for consistent linking of that interpretation across subjects. If such an approach could be developed, then not only would the learning processes be supported in all subjects; students would also be seeing the world of knowledge through the themes in a consistent yet challenging manner.

Reporting learning in the IPC

One challenge for schools is how to reconcile their reporting system with assessment. The IPC is a well-documented and well-supported curriculum. Armed with the approach of Looking for Learning, schools can gather strong evidence of learning and thus provide for students as they progress as learners. Many primary schools avoid the usual pitfalls associated with reporting by using narratives and other forms that avoid more traditional representations such as grading. This is not always possible though; nor is it seen as acceptable by some schools. This is an area in which the IPC could perhaps assist schools. With access to a large school network, it may be possible to find examples that reflect a standards-based reporting approach and thus empower schools to facilitate change.

If reporting is not treated as part of the learning feedback process then educational best practice can be subverted. For example, if while professing to support differentiated instruction a grading system is used, particularly one where data is collected in the form of numbers and presented in a grade book system, then the objective is undermined. The question of how reporting supports learning is one that is as much a political issue as an educational issue for schools. Just because it would be tough to change the *status quo* does not mean that the question should not be addressed. Here, the support and guidance of the IPC organisation would be of great value. This is a battleground for the very brave and for a school to embark upon changes alone would be a daunting task. Leadership from IPC and Fieldwork Education, as has been provided in the past, would be welcome.

Schools need modelling and guidance on how to provide a 'standards-based' reporting approach in schools. Part of the challenge is to build into the structure acceptance and recognition that all students have a spread of abilities in the learning targets identified as age-appropriate. Educators therefore have to expect that students will have achieved age level targets, below age level targets and above age level targets. Thinking of learning as exclusively an age or year level phenomenon is reinforced by reporting systems. Schools need to go beyond this if student learning is to be truly represented in report systems. Because of the level of politics involved in such a process (amongst teachers and with the parent community), leadership from the IPC would be of enormous value.

Internationalism and the IPC

Learning targets that promote an international perspective are something of which the IPC is rightly proud. To say that all students should develop an international perspective as part of their education is valuable, particularly in the context of the increasing effects of globalisation. More and more parents are seeing the value of this component of the IPC. For international schools, it is a reaffirmation of what they normally do. The existence of learning targets means that it is not an incidental or osmotic process. Rather, it is a deliberate strategy to develop student knowledge and understanding, and to shape attitudes and perceptions – thus strengthening the nature of international schools, as well as the international dimension of IPC schools in state systems.

Let us now consider the emerging situation in China. In the last three years our school has been approached by Chinese teachers and educational leaders to assist them with understanding international education. The Chinese teachers and administrators are being asked by educational authorities to explore this form of education as a basis for the future development of Chinese education. What does this mean? If we look at the IPC from the position of a Chinese educator we make an interesting discovery. While all of the IPC documentation could be translated into Chinese, if the translated version were given to Chinese teachers they would have no idea what to do. We have tried to work with Chinese teachers who have visited our school, observed classes, and engaged in discussions about the curriculum and the pedagogy, and their reaction is always the same. They do not understand what is going on. They are fascinated and can often see the intent and potential value, but the approach is alien to them.

Herein lies the problem. What this experience demonstrates is that the way in which we develop, write and implement our curriculum reflects our culture. The extent of the cultural factor is so significant that it seems to dominate the way we develop all of our curricula. If someone from a very different culture, yet trained in the same profession, cannot understand what to do when the curriculum is presented, then the difference must be enormous. When teachers in an international school read the IPC documentation, they know what they have to do. Implicit in the documentation is the myriad of pedagogical approaches and philosophical positions that teachers in international schools recognise and accept. The way the IPC is written makes it easy for a teacher to implement, unless they are from a significantly different culture from that generally found in international schools. Students in international schools know what is happening and why, because this is part of their cultural experience – which makes it easier for the teacher to implement the curriculum. If a Chinese-speaking international teacher were to be placed in a Chinese class and try to use the pedagogy and curriculum of the IPC it would not work.

The challenge is this: for China to incorporate Western pedagogy into its system would mean a significant change, and would involve teachers being able to draw upon a curriculum such as the IPC. As it stands the IPC is non-transferable, though its adoption in China may be possible under certain conditions. Chinese educators, at this stage, are seeking to understand our teaching methods. We talk to them about differentiated instruction, authentic assessment, multiple intelligences, standards and benchmarks, rubrics, group work, learning and so on. None of these concepts and approaches is known to them. In a recent meeting I presented Bloom's Taxonomy and it was a revelation. The teachers and administrators loved the ideas and immediately wanted to understand the details. There is a strong desire to learn and change. As these educators come to grips with what we do, though, they have to retain the integrity of their culture. Recently I made a presentation to 200 Chinese heads of school and the education minister, and in conclusion I made the following remark which resonated strongly with the audience:

"The curriculum and pedagogy that we use reflects very strongly our culture. If any attempt were made to transpose this into Chinese schools it would fail. What should happen is for Chinese educators to learn about what we do and why. Then, select the components that are deemed to be of value and re-shape them to be Chinese in nature."

Only by shaping the curriculum and pedagogy through the filter of the culture will something emerge that is valid and could be implemented in Chinese schools. As this process continues, Chinese educators will see the role of curriculum documentation and, in particular, how pedagogy, assessment and learning can be built into curriculum documentation. Because IPC is such a strong example of best practice in Western education, it would be fascinating to see how it could be used as a foundation for a very different style of curriculum, holding onto the core elements yet at the same time reflecting a different viewpoint. If this could work in China then it would surely be an applicable perspective for any other cultural context. Thus, internationalism takes a different form. Not only could the IPC promote the learning of internationalism; it could also become more international in nature. I am not suggesting that this would be an easy challenge, but it is certainly a point worth contemplating.

Conclusion

I believe that the IPC, and hopefully the new International Middle Years Curriculum, will continue to evolve and promote best practice. The opportunity exists, however, for these curricula to become even more significant in promoting exceptional education in schools through modelling, refinement of curriculum, providing leadership in difficult areas of implementation and taking on new challenges. If we see IPC as already complete then we fall into the trap of complacency. We are constantly learning about education, best practice and how to link learning to individuals, cultures, curriculum, assessment and reporting. There is no fixed answer, nor should there be. Once any curriculum becomes institutionalised there is a risk that it will ossify and become defensive about suggested change. The premise of IPC is that learning is paramount and, by definition, learning is a process of change. That IPC needs continually to change is important to recognise. It is a leading example of what can and should be done in education. How and where IPC develops will depend upon research, documentation of best practice and political will to encourage the continuation of change as the constant.

Postscript

Martin Skelton

The question 'where does the IPC go from here?' is not a new one. It's a question we have been asking from the very beginning, with the result that the 2012 IPC is a very different thing altogether from the 2000 version that was first made available to schools. It is bigger and broader for a start. You will have read in this volume about the growth from an original 40 units of work from which schools could choose, to the 80+ units now available. Back in 2000 there was no assessment for learning programme, no specialist subject learning programmes for art, music, physical education and ICT, no package of membership services, no professional development programme, no summer school or regional summer schools, no magazine, no self-review and accreditation protocol, and no online route planner. All of these things have been developed in the last ten years, along with a three-times updated website and range of online services. If your last glimpse of the IPC as curriculum product was in 2000, you would hardly recognise it now.

More importantly, it is much deeper now than it was in 2000 as our awareness of what we are doing has deepened. Running a video of some of the early training sessions would be a little like reviewing those photos of ourselves as teenagers. We recognise who we were but we can't quite believe what we looked like. We have learned a huge amount over the past 12 years, which is why all of the units and the teacher guidance have been updated (again) very recently. Back then, we knew that international-mindedness was important but I'm not ashamed to say that I don't think any of us knew what we meant by that. We were truly – to use one of our own assessment-for-learning terms – at beginning level. We are much more confident now about what international-mindedness can be, and how we can incorporate that into a curriculum in a coherent way that helps teachers help children develop this important disposition and the equally important skills that run alongside it. I am not saying here that we are right, because 'right' is a notion that is applicable to knowledge but not to skills or understanding, and it is our understanding of international-mindedness that has deepened over the past 12 years. Our view of understanding continues to be controversial to some, and we continue to challenge it ourselves. But we know teachers find it helpful in making more sense of children's learning and their own practice. We are confident that our understanding of what international-mindedness might be is based on much firmer foundations than it was in 2000.

The previous paragraph reflects the way in which our work with schools, children and students over the past 12 years has given us depth about the process of learning, too. We have a much more coherent view than we did then that knowledge, skills and understanding are each learned, taught and assessed differently. We are confident that an awareness and appreciation of these differences has a significant impact on learning in the classroom and on how a curriculum can help teachers facilitate great learning. That's why it is one of the criteria of our self-review and accreditation protocol. All of this is to say that we continue to ask the questions 'how can the IPC do a better job of helping teachers help children to learn as well as they can?', 'how can we help children to learn those things that will equip them to live successfully in the 21st century?' and 'how can we help children to learn in a way that engages them so much that they will remember how exciting learning can be for the rest of their lives?'

What might the next ten years of changes bring? As a 'product' the curriculum will almost certainly look very different. It's hard to believe that in ten years' time hard copies of the IPC will be delivered to schools. Given that only five years ago few of us owned or had heard of 'tablet computers' I will not attempt to predict what the delivery mechanism will be, but I can't see it being a big heavy box delivered by slow-mail. Technology will drive the identity and actions of our IPC community, too. The current community of IPC member schools just amazes me. There are already member schools in different countries working together, sharing and co-creating learning, and there are single country self-help groups working together to help to improve learning in their schools with only minimum help from us at the centre. But technology is going to make so many changes to how IPC members work together. It's probably true to say that, at the time of writing this postscript, our use and development of social media in ways that benefit both teachers and students, and allow for greater cooperation between member schools and individual teachers, school principals, parents and others, has been slower than we would have wished. But we already know from other schools we work with how many exciting things can happen through the use of different social media. I suspect that by the time this book is published we will already be linking people together electronically and digitally in ways that aren't the case at the time of writing. Who knows what ten years' time will look like? I hope for a fully interconnected community, including the central IPC team that is learning from each other testing out new ideas and refining approaches, researching together and creating even greater learning, teaching and fun. To close these thoughts about technology, I can't ignore the impact that apps will have on learning over the next two or three years, let alone ten. As we have thought hard about the differences between knowledge, skills and understanding, it seems clear that apps and different programmes have a huge part to play in helping children to learn and consolidate the knowledge that we believe to be important; that they have some part to play in developing both subject skills and life skills (perhaps through gaming) and, probably, less part to play in enabling the reflection that leads to understanding.

What the IPC looks like, of course, is determined by what the IPC is trying to do. The early 20th century mantra of architects and designers, that 'form follows function', continues to be true (and a good example of one of the big ideas of our International Middle Years Curriculum that 'it's important to honour behaviour and processes that have proven merit'). I don't think the central purpose of the IPC – enshrined in our tag line as 'great learning, great teaching and great fun' – will change that much. But what that means, how broad its scope is, and what the IPC can actually deliver and what it can't is going to have to be a really important focus for us. Hopefully, it is going to be supported and fuelled by research that takes place at different levels. At the moment, research into the impact and success of the IPC is in its infancy. Generally speaking, we receive fantastic feedback from our member schools, teachers, children and their parents. But ever since my own university days the idea of the 'Hawthorne effect', in which a newly-introduced procedure or product can benefit from a positive but short-lived response, has haunted me. We need to be continually aware that the good feedback the IPC receives has to be supported and researched on an ongoing basis.

This book, and the slowly growing number of IPC-related research projects that students at masters and doctorate level are now beginning to undertake, are the beginning of what I hope will be a long and rigorous research tradition that tests what the IPC claims to offer, critiques it rigorously and supports its ongoing development. Every contribution in this book is personal but each contribution is personal out of experience; each contribution raises notions that we can investigate to see whether it is true or not, for whom and where. We have much to research. The IPC self-review and accreditation protocol sets out the nine criteria that form the heart of the IPC. Even though some of those criteria are shared with other curricula around the world I hope that, if nothing else happens, the next ten years will produce a body of research that is focused on what we claim to be important about our curriculum. There are a few areas of research that I think are particularly important. I will choose just four for now.

We claim that one of the outcomes of learning through the IPC is that our children will develop what we believe to be an essential 21st century quality: the ability to see things from different perspectives. The design of the IPC reflects this, most clearly where we ask schools to help children learn (for instance) science through Chocolate, history through Chocolate, geography through Chocolate, and so on. For us, this is the opposite of being modern or glib; it is a part of what 21st century rigour looks like. Our intention is that we will provide children with such experiences that, when asked the question later in life, 'So what do you think about the situation in Afghanistan?', they will automatically fall to answering, 'Do you mean, politically, socially, culturally or economically?' In a complex world, multiple perspectives (combined with the ability to weigh them and come to a conclusion) are crucial. Given that we think this, it is vital that we find out just how possible it is for primary children and in what areas it is possible. We set out to be challenging and rigorous, but we can only do this well if we know the boundaries within which we can act.

(No amount of rigorous activity and encouragement will help a two-month-old to walk. We are much better waiting and putting our energies elsewhere.)

I hope we will benefit from significant research into a better awareness of what understanding is and how it develops in primary-aged children. The IPC commits to its importance; it features clearly in all of our learning outcomes. But we struggle, along with colleagues and teachers in our member schools and other schools with which we work, to define what it means and what it looks like. As we have developed a better idea of what understanding is in relation to knowledge and skills, we know that we need further clarity about whether understanding in mathematics, for instance, is the same sort of learning as understanding in art, geography or other subjects. We need to develop a sense of how the relatively late development of the prefrontal cortex (almost always after the end of primary schooling) impacts on the potential for understanding in primary children. We know that 'understanding' is important, but we are conscious of the danger of taking it for granted and paying lip service to it. No curriculum that sets out to help children achieve 'great learning' can afford to do that.

My third choice lies around the difficult question of the knowledge, skills and dispositions that people will need to be 'successful' in the 21st century. This was the very first question we asked ourselves, and many others, right at the beginning of the IPC's development. It is a difficult question because no-one can know the answer; as contexts change, the qualities we need to deal with them change. But flunking the question is not possible either. It was obvious to us from the beginning, and is even more so now, that so many questions flow from an answer to this question and that without answers a curriculum has no chance of coherence. We are very proud of the IPC, but we also know that it is a tool that helps teachers help students learn. We know it isn't the star of the show, but rather part of the foundations. What a curriculum looks like and contains should be an answer to the question of what help teachers and schools need in order to provide children with the learning they need. So 'what do they need?' is the starting question, and an answer can only be furnished by a mix of research and hard reflection. If what the IPC is fundamentally about changes in the future it will have to be because children's needs have changed.

My final choice for a greater research base to support the IPC is in the area of international-mindedness. I know that this is already a well-researched area in part, and much of the research has helped us focus our view of the development of international-mindedness around Howard Gardner's lovely phrase, 'a declining sense of egocentricity'. However, the IPC needs more research about the intercultural interpretations of the kinds of academic, social, emotional and physical learning the IPC tries to develop. The very origination of the IPC, as you will have read in Chapter One of this book, was to provide a curriculum capable of developing learning for children of many different nationalities. My own thoughts are that this presents relatively few problems in the area of subject skills which seem to feature in the curriculums of many different cultures. Knowledge, on the other hand, is technically the easiest outcome to learn, but is problematic internationally because it often represents the cultural identity of different countries. We need help to determine what knowledge can be common across cultures and what cultures need to decide for themselves. Currently, I am not remotely confident that understanding has a common base in my own culture. We need to know urgently what it means in different cultural contexts.

Reviewing what I have written here, three final thoughts come to mind. First, the IPC has never stood still; not for one second. Our members and my colleagues would never allow it. Second, we should take satisfaction that we are properly struggling to produce a curriculum that is founded on helping children learn for the 21st century rather than on simply providing activities for them to do in the classroom. Finally, I realise why it has been such fun and so rewarding. Who, interested in making an impact on children's learning, could want to be involved in anything better than this?